Terrorism, Legitimacy, and Power

Essays by

Irving Louis Horowitz
Anthony C. E. Quainton
Yehezkel Dror
Conor Cruise O'Brien
Paul Wilkinson
Robert Cox

 Wesleyan University Press
Middletown, Connecticut

Edited by

Martha Crenshaw

Terrorism, Legitimacy, and Power

The Consequences of Political Violence

First Edition

Published by Wesleyan University Press, 110 Mt. Vernon Street, Middletown, Connecticut 06457

Distributed by Harper & Row, Publishers, Keystone Industrial Park, Scranton, Pennsylvania 18512

First printing, 1983; second printing, 1984

All inquiries and permissions requests should be addressed to the Publisher, Wesleyan University Press, 110 Mt. Vernon Street, Middletown, Connecticut 06457

LIBRARY OF CONGRESS CATALOGING PUBLICATION DATA
Main entry under title:

Terrorism, legitimacy, and power
"[Based on] a symposium, 'Terrorism: the challenge to the state,' held in January 1982 to commemorate the sesquicentennial anniversary of the founding of Wesleyan University"—Editor's pref.
Bibliography: p.
Includes index.
1. Terrorism—Congresses. 2. Violence—Congresses.
3. Terrorism—Northern Ireland—Congresses. 4. Terrorism—Argentina—Congresses. 5. Power (Social sciences)—
1. Crenshaw, Martha

HV 6431.T48 1982 303.6'25 82-23756
ISBN 0-8195-5081-7

Manufactured in the United States of America

Editor's Preface

The essays contained in this volume are the products of a symposium, "Terrorism: The Challenge to the State," held in January 1982 to commemorate the sesquicentennial anniversary of the founding of Wesleyan University. The conference, one in a series of sesquicentennial symposia on important public issues, focused on the impact of terrorism on state, society, and individual, particularly the dilemma it poses for liberal democracy. Participants included Wesleyan alumni, students, and faculty, as well as outside guests. In addition to the authors who presented the papers included in this volume, Roy Tucker, President of Risks International, Inc., Alexandria, Virginia, led an informal seminar on the effects of terrorism on business. Anthony Quainton, as well as presenting a paper, held a seminar on American policy toward terrorism. For the publication of this collection, the authors have revised their original presentations to take into account the comments and criticisms generated in the lively discussions that were an integral part of the symposium.

The success of the symposium depended first on the commitment, the intellectual initiative, and the cooperativeness of the authors, whose contributions provide new and stimulating analyses of the problem of terrorism. The active participation of those who conducted seminars or attended the symposium added significantly to its achievements. I would like to thank Joseph W. Reed, Professor of English and Chairman of the Sesquicentennial Committee, for his advice and support. Ian Harvey, Zena Temkin, and Joseph Alter were invaluable administrative assistants. President and Mrs. Colin G. Campbell,

Oliver W. Holmes, Ann M. Wightman, John G. Grumm, and Richard W. Boyd also deserve special thanks. Finally, I am grateful for the aid of Lee Messina, who typed large portions of the manuscript, and of Jeannette Hopkins, Editor of the Wesleyan University Press.

MARTHA CRENSHAW

Middletown, Connecticut

Contents

Notes on the Contributors

Robert Cox is associate editor of the Charleston News and Courier and former editor of the Buenos Aires Herald. He received the Maria Moors Cabot Prize from Columbia University in 1978 and was made an officer of the Order of the British Empire in 1979. While a guest scholar at the Wilson Center of the Smithsonian Institution in 1980, he wrote The Sound of One Hand Clapping: A Preliminary Study of the Argentine Press in a Time of Terror.

Martha Crenshaw is Associate Professor of Government at Wesleyan University and, in 1982–83, a Fellow at the Russell Sage Foundation in New York. She is the author of Revolutionary Terrorism: The FLN in Algeria, 1954–1962.

Yehezkel Dror is Professor of Political Science and Wolfson Professor of Public Administration at the Hebrew University of Jerusalem. He is the author of Crazy States: A Counterconventional Strategic Problem, Public Policymaking Reexamined: A Second Look, and many other works in the field of policy analysis. In addition to his academic work, he was a senior staff member of the Rand Corporation in 1978–80, and served as Senior Planning and Policy Analysis Advisor of the Israeli Ministry of Defense, 1975–77.

Irving Louis Horowitz is Hannah Arendt Distinguished Professor of Sociology and Political Science at Rutgers University. He is editor-in-chief of Transaction/Society and the author of numerous books, most recently, Taking Lives: Genocide and State Power, Ideology and Utopia in the United States, and Beyond Empire and Revolution: Militarization and Consolidation in the Third World.

Conor Cruise O'Brien is the former editor of The Observer (London). He is a former member of the Irish Dail, 1969–

77, and Minister of Posts and Telegraphs, 1973–77. He was Schweitzer Professor of Humanities at New York University, 1965–69, and Visiting Fellow at Nuffield College, Oxford, 1972–75. He is the author of numerous books, plays, and articles, among which are *States of Ireland* and *Herod: Reflections on Political Violence.*

Anthony C. E. Quainton, a career Foreign Service officer, is United States Ambassador to Nicaragua. He was the Director of the Department of State's Office for Combatting Terrorism, 1978–81, and Ambassador to the Central African Empire, 1976–78.

Paul Wilkinson is Professor of International Relations at the University of Aberdeen, Scotland. He is the author of *Social Movement, Political Terrorism, Terrorism and the Liberal State,* and *The New Fascists.* He recently edited *British Perspectives on Terrorism.*

Terrorism, Legitimacy, and Power

Martha Crenshaw

1

Introduction: Reflections on the Effects of Terrorism[1]

The Meaning of Terrorism

As Yehezkel Dror observes in his paper in this volume, the varied usages of the term "terrorism," though a barrier to intellectual exchange, are worthy of study in themselves. Although it is by no means easy to isolate and differentiate meanings, there seems to be an analytically useful distinction between *normative* and *analytical* definitions.

Conor Cruise O'Brien's interpretation is firmly based on political values from which he derives rigorous standards for judging political action. He defines terrorism in terms of the political context in which it occurs, seeing terrorism as unjustified violence against a democratic state that permits effective and peaceful forms of opposition. Thus a black activist who bombs a police station in South Africa is not a terrorist; the Provisional Irish Republican Army (IRA) bomber of a Brit-

1. I should like to thank Paul Wilkinson, Stephen Sloan, and Richard Boyd for their comments on this essay.

ish military barracks is. Identical acts performed in different situations do not fall under the same definition.

The danger inherent in the normative definition is that it verges on the polemical. If "terrorist" is what one calls one's opponent (regardless of whether or not one's friend is a "freedom fighter"), then the word is more of an epithet or a debating stratagem than a label that enables all who read it, whatever their ideological affiliation, to know what terrorism is and what it is not.

The value of the normative approach is that it confronts squarely a critical problem in the analysis of terrorism, and indeed any form of political violence: the issue of legitimacy. Terrorists of the left deny the legitimacy of the state and claim that the use of violence against it is morally justified. Terrorists of the right deny the legitimacy of opposition and hold that violence in the service of order is sanctioned by the values of the status quo. As Anthony Quainton emphasizes in his essay, an imperative for the state response to terrorism is to maintain and defend its legitimacy while delegitimizing the terrorist challenge. Nor will Robert Cox in his insistent report on the tragic events in Argentina let us forget that violence means injury and death to human beings. The need for scholarly objectivity and abstraction does not excuse us from the obligation to judge the morality of the use of force, whether by the state or against it.

Is the place for judgment, however, in the construction of a definition? It seems preferable to establish a neutral descriptive definition, general enough to be applicable to the circumstances of both South Africa and Northern Ireland, and only then to make value judgments about different cases. Such a basic definition would include the following attributes: the systematic use of unorthodox political violence by small conspiratorial groups with the purpose of manipulating political attitudes rather than physically defeating an enemy. The intent of terrorist violence is psychological and symbolic, not material. Terrorism is premeditated and purposeful violence, employed in a struggle for political power. As Harold Lasswell defined it: "Terrorists are participants in the political process who strive for political results by arousing acute anxieties."[2]

So defined, terrorism may be found in both democratic and authoritarian regimes, but moral distinctions can be made based upon the context in which terrorism is used. We may accept the criteria of consent and participation proposed by Conor Cruise O'Brien or we may expand them. Terrorism can be judged on two levels: the morality of the ends and the morality of the means.[3]

First, are the goals of the terrorists democratic or nondemocratic? That is, is their aim to create or perpetuate a regime of privilege and inequality, to deny liberty to other people, or to further ends of justice, freedom, and equality? We feel differently about the actions of the People's Will, which sought to replace the Russian autocracy with a constitutional regime, than we do about the Klu Klux Klan or about the Orange extremists of Northern Ireland.

Second, terrorism undertaken to combat demonstrable injustice, especially a threat to the survival of a community, is more justifiable than that which is not. We would not, for example, have disapproved of the use of terrorism by the Jews against the Nazi regime. We would, however, repudiate the terrorism of the Red Army Fraction against the Federal Republic of Germany, which, although not a perfect democracy, is not demonstrably unjust.

A third criterion of ends qualifies these propositions. Terrorism must not, as far as the terrorists can foresee, result in *worse* injustice than the condition the terrorists oppose. This

2. "Terrorism and the Political Process," *Terrorism: An International Journal* 1 (1978): 255.
3. This analysis of the issue of justification for violence is based on several sources. Of these, three deal specifically with the morality of terrorism: Michael Walzer, *Just and Unjust Wars* (New York: Basic Books, 1977), chapter 12; and Anthony Arblaster's review article, "Terrorism: Myths, Meaning and Morals," *Political Studies* 5 (1977): 413–24. (Walzer's argument stands in contrast to the one presented here.) Also of interest is Albert Camus, "Le terrorisme individuel," in *L'homme révolté*, reprinted in *Essais* (Paris: Gallimard, 1962). Other sources include Ernest van den Haag, *Political Violence and Civil Disobedience* (New York: Harper and Row, 1972), and Ted Honderich, *Political Violence* (Ithaca: Cornell University Press, 1976).

argument would counter Conor Cruise O'Brien's position, which denies that the French Resistance was a terrorist organization because it opposed an oppressive enemy. The French Resistance, primarily its communist elements, did occasionally resort to terrorism as defined in this essay. Resistance and partisan groups in other European nations used terrorism more frequently. In most cases the use of terrorism by the Resistance was not justified, because it provoked the Nazi occupation to horrible retaliations against innocent civilians. Once the Resistance leaders knew that the Nazis were capable of murdering the entire population of a village such as Oradour-sur-Glane, whose inhabitants were selected only because of their physical proximity to the scene of assassinations of German soldiers, then the Resistance was not justified in further acts of terrorism. It is one thing to risk one's life in the service of a cause, another to risk the lives of people who have no choice in the matter.

The morality of the means of terrorism is also open to judgment. The targets of terrorism are morally significant; witness the difference between material objects and human casualties. We are more likely to approve the Front de Libération du Québec's (FLQ) blowing up a statue of General Wolf than their kidnapping and assassination of Pierre Laporte. Furthermore, two types of victims of terrorism may be distinguished according to the degree of their responsibility. This is not merely a question of numbers of victims but of selectivity. Victims may be individuals who are harmful to the terrorists because they are decision-makers or uniformed agents who are responsible for the state of injustice the terrorists combat. On the other hand, citizens of the state, with no public role, or citizens of other states who have negligible influence over the policies of the offending state, are harmless, although passive obedience to the rules of an unjust regime incurs some moral responsibility. We may also judge as morally unacceptable terrorist attacks on members of a social class which they regard as oppressive, such as "colonialists," "imperialists," or simply the "bourgeoisie." We would therefore distinguish sharply between the Irgun Zvai Leumi's attacks on British soldiers and the Popular Front for the Liberation of Palestine's violence against airline passengers traveling to Israel.

In sum, we can develop a neutral definition of terrorism while retaining the ability to make moral judgments about its use in different political circumstances. Labeling an action "terrorist" is not in itself a moral claim. There may also be an important relationship between the justifiability of terrorism and its political effectiveness—a question that will be explored further in this essay.

The Effects of Terrorism

As Irving Louis Horowitz argues in his essay on the routinization of terrorism, most analyses have emphasized the causes and forms rather than the consequences of terrorism. Studies of government policies toward terrorism have also proliferated.[4] Yet the outcomes of campaigns of terrorism have been largely ignored. Such a neglect of results, broadly conceived, is characteristic of studies of political violence in general.[5] The essays in this volume, however, are linked by their attention to the social and political effects of terrorism, particularly its impact on democratic institutions and values. Each author implicitly or explicitly directs our notice to the need to determine precisely and concretely what the effects of terrorism are in different circumstances. Does terrorism produce change? If so, in what direction, with what intensity, and how rapidly?

An initial problem in assessing the results of terrorism is that it is never the unique causal factor leading to identifiable outcomes. The intermingling of social and political effects with other events and trends makes terrorism difficult to isolate. It is clear, for example, that Yehezkel Dror's assumption that democracies are increasingly under strain is widely shared.

4. See, for example, Robert Kupperman and Darrell Trent, *Terrorism: Threat, Reality, Response* (Stanford: Hoover Institution Press, 1979).
5. This is noted by Ted Robert Gurr in "On the Outcomes of Violent Conflict," in Ted Robert Gurr, ed., *Handbook of Political Conflict: Theory and Research* (New York: Free Press, 1980), pp. 238–94.

But the role terrorism plays in democracy's predicament is dis-
puted. The authors represented here disagree among themselves; some, like Yehezkel Dror, feel that terrorism is a minor
part of the crisis; others, like Paul Wilkinson and Conor Cruise
O'Brien, see it as a much more serious threat; Irving Louis Horowitz argues that the state's response to terrorism is more
dangerous to democracy than is terrorism itself.

Moreover, terrorism is a dynamic process. Not only is its
causal role difficult to distinguish from those of other phenomena, but its effects are diffused and modified over time. Un-
detectable processes of incremental change resulting from the
interactions between terrorists and governments, mixed with
myriad other changes, may be more serious than the immediately visible consequences that generate most public concern. Terrorism may be important although it occurs long
before the climactic events we often identify as determinants
of major change.

The subject of the effects of terrorism is so complex and so
multifaceted that we can only sketch here an outline of where
changes might occur. An initial distinction, underscored by
Horowitz's analysis, is between social and political changes,
which are the focus of this discussion.[6] Terrorism may transform the fundamental character of society and government
through genuinely revolutionary changes or, more commonly,
may result in changes that appear relatively minor but that
nonetheless may alter the character of the state. Furthermore,
the results of terrorism are interrelated and subject to feedback
effects. The outcome of terrorism affects the future of terrorism.
For example, terrorism can provoke government repression,
which in turn stimulates further terrorism, which provokes
more repression. To complicate the analysis, the effects of terrorism are rarely limited to the state in which terrorism occurs.

6. As Roy Tucker emphasized during the symposium, terrorism has not
greatly altered global business investment patterns. The localized impact in
areas such as Northern Ireland or the Basque provinces of Spain, however, has
been severe. See Susanna W. Purnell and Eleanor S. Wainstein, *The Problems of
U.S. Businesses Operating Abroad in Terrorist Environments* (Santa Monica:
Rand, 1981).

Terrorism vividly demonstrates the global interdependence of nations, as both Irving Louis Horowitz and Anthony Quainton point out.

Political Effects

Terrorism can contribute to change in four areas: the overall distribution of political power; government policies, especially as they affect civil liberties; the political behavior of citizens; and the prospects for the continuation of violence.

The structure of power. Terrorism may result in radical changes in power relationships within a state, involving major shifts in who governs and under what rules. Terrorism can lead to the replacement of one government by another composed of new elites ruling by different constitutional principles.

Most obviously, terrorism has been an important part of successful struggles for independence from foreign domination. The termination of the British Mandate in Palestine and the French withdrawal from Algeria are prominent examples. In both cases the colonial metropolis relinquished its hold on a colony rather than fight an endless war. Terrorism, combined with guerrilla warfare and mass mobilization against the occupier, was significant in making each conflict essentially unwinnable for the colonial power. We might place Kenya, Cyprus, Aden, and Vietnam in this category.

Second, terrorism has resulted in indigenous transfers of power from one regime to another. In Uruguay, Argentina, and Turkey, terrorism was instrumental in the overthrow of a civilian government by a military dictatorship pledged to halt terrorism its predecessor had proved unable to control. Robert Cox also argues that terrorism was a factor in returning Juan Peron to power in Argentina, which substituted an erratic dictatorship for relatively benign military rule. Revolutions have also been preceded by terrorism, as in Russia, Iran, and Nicaragua; the complex relationship between terrorism and revolutionary change requires further study before propositions can be made about its nature.

Terrorism appears to produce substantial change in government in a third way, by creating conditions that provoke the intervention of an outside power. In Northern Ireland, for example, IRA terrorism instigated the British imposition of direct rule in 1972. The result was the demise of the politically autonomous Stormont regime. A more dramatic case is Lebanon, now a striking example of a Hobbesian state of anarchy. Palestinian terrorism against Israel led to Israeli retaliation against Lebanon and the Palestinian enclaves that sought sanctuary there. Israeli raids and occupation of Lebanese territory combined with the domestic impact of the Palestinian issue on the delicate balance of Lebanese politics destroyed the political system and brought about Syrian intervention.

The fact that none of these fallen regimes was a democracy should comfort those persuaded by Yehezkel Dror's view that democracies are not fragile but vigorously healthy. Uruguay, the most democratic of the overthrown regimes, was an oligarchy beset not only by terrorism but by severe economic problems.[7] On balance, terrorism assists in the demise of regimes already distressed; yet, we must admit that democracy has not gained as a result of many recent changes of regime. Only in Northern Ireland could we say that the shift in the locus of official power from Belfast to London furthered the ends of democracy.

Radical change, however, is rare. Terrorism tends more often to produce less profound changes in the domestic configuration of political power. It can produce redistribution of power within a governing elite as well as minor shifts in the balance of power between the terrorist challengers and the regime. A faction or bureaucracy, as for example, the military, the police, or an intelligence agency, may gain power. Institutional changes, such as the coordination of U.S. policy through the State Department's Office for Combatting Terrorism, which Anthony Quainton describes, and the establishment of elite intervention units in the military and police, may or may not

---

7. For example, Arturo C. Porzecanski, *Uruguay's Tupamaros: The Urban Guerrilla* (New York: Praeger, 1973).

reflect altered power relations. There is also the possibility of a greater centralization of power as a consequence of a national government's preempting local authorities in responding to terrorism.

Of minor changes in political power, however, the most serious appears to be fragmentation, not centralization, of power. A diffusion of power is seen, for example, in the emergence of clandestine counterterrorist vigilantes or paramilitary organizations posing as defenders of the established order. The connection between counterterrorist groups and the government is usually ambiguous. There appear to be two patterns of reactionary counterterrorism, depending on the degree of the government's complicity. In the first case, government security forces act secretly and unofficially, thus not bound by legality, with the knowledge and consent if not the direction of official political leaders. The second pattern involves much less central control. The counterterrorist organizations are essentially private although their members are often recruited from the police and military and benefit from assistance from within the security forces. Private counterterrorists may then turn against the government if it is perceived as insufficiently loyal to the cause of maintaining the status quo or lax in combating terrorism.

Extensive government involvement apparently prevailed in Argentina and Brazil and still characterizes Guatemala and El Salvador, although El Salvador represents an ominous combination of both types of counterterrorism. A pattern of counterterrorist autonomy was seen during the latter years of the Algerian War in the Secret Army Organization and in the interwar period in Germany and Italy. The Protestant extremists analyzed by Paul Wilkinson also fall into this category. In such cases the government finds itself combating two extremisms, with political power divided among three centers. The government is no longer an arbitrator, but becomes engaged in the struggle for power.

The international configuration of power, however, has changed little as a result of terrorism. Some authors and American public officials insist that the secret sponsorship of terrorism by the Soviet Union is an asset in the Cold War confrontation, but this assertion is questionable. Terrorism is not a prerogative of Soviet-inspired revolutionism; it is, for instance, the favored device of the Islamic fundamentalist organization, known as the Muslim Brotherhood, in its opposition to the Soviet Union's ally, Syria. The hostage crisis in Iran, where terrorism stemmed from indigenous radicalism, not Soviet-inspired subversion, is considered to have damaged the power position of the United States. The sponsorship of terrorism has earned both Iran and Libya the enmity of the United States but has not otherwise discernibly affected the international status quo. Cuba's responsibility for terrorism in Latin America, despite the Reagan administration's charges, seems to have little basis in fact, as Robert Cox notes with respect to Argentina, in particular, and to the general movement in Latin America from rural guerrilla warfare to urban terrorism.

Government policies. The policy changes resulting from terrorism have been subjected to more scrutiny than other effects because the short-term efficacy of government performance concerns policy-makers more than long-term consequences. Both government actions to destroy the terrorist group and attempts to protect potential targets from terrorist assault can result in the curtailing of civil liberties.

The predominant thrust of offensive policies against terrorism is hard-line. Notwithstanding Anthony Quainton's complaint that some governments remain pusillanimous, after an initial period of adjustment few governments have found terrorism tolerable. Before the tactic of seizing hostages for ransom became routine—and this form of bargaining originally represented a significant innovation in terrorist methods—certain governments, Mexico and West Germany among them, were inclined to grant terrorist demands. The strong tendency that has emerged over time, however, is a response based on "no concessions"; West Germany, for example, changed its policy in 1975. A widely accepted if unproven "lesson" of terrorism is that granting terrorist demands encourages more terrorism.[8]

Governments threatened by terrorism have not neglected to refine the implementation of offensive strategies, such as improving intelligence capabilities, sharpening psychological negotiation techniques, and establishing elite antiterrorist commando squads for rescue operations. The judicial response has been reformed to expand the definition of a punishable crime to include all forms of terrorist violence.

Intelligence is often considered the key to combating terrorism, but the government's need to obtain information sometimes confuses the relationship between terrorists and authorities. The best source of information about terrorist plans is, of course, the terrorists themselves. Captured terrorists may be persuaded to talk through plea-bargaining tactics or be tortured into talking if the regime is sufficiently oblivious to humanitarian issues. The government may also infiltrate the terrorist organization, an option that tempts governments of all dispositions. The result is inevitable control difficulties with the counteragent, or *agent-provocateur*, of whom the most famous was the Russian Asev, who, while in the pay of the Russian secret service, headed the terrorist branch of the Socialist-Revolutionary party. A recent example of the ambiguous relationship between acquiring intelligence and participating in terrorism is the aid furnished by former American CIA operatives for Libyan terrorist training.

The most visible symbol of government watchfulness in protecting citizens from terrorism is the upgraded security service at airports to prevent hijackings. Physical security measures extend to thorough searches of individuals and their belongings and to sealing national borders, depending upon the gravity and

8. On the results of resisting or acceding to explicit terrorist demands, see Brian Jenkins, Janera Johnson, and David Ronfeldt, *Numbered Lives: Some Statistical Observations from 77 International Hostage Episodes* (Santa Monica: Rand, 1977); and Brian M. Jenkins, *Embassies under Siege: A Review of 48 Embassy Takeovers, 1971–1980* (Santa Monica: Rand, 1981). In general, little positive correlation is found between government concessions and vulnerability to future terrorism.

the source of the terrorist threat. But because the opportunities for terrorism, especially bombings, are everywhere, governments cannot possibly protect all vulnerable targets. There is also a limit to public tolerance of security measures.

There is some debate over whether or not governments should respond to terrorism with policies designed to eradicate its sources. Anthony Quainton argues that in their concentration on immediate security measures, governments should not forget that the causes of terrorism often lie in political and social conditions of discrimination, inequality, and deprivation. Yehezkel Dror strongly disagrees, insisting that because the causes of terrorism are multiple and unknowable, governments can only deal with the physical manifestation of underlying discontent.

Have governments realistically chosen to respond to terrorism by dealing with causes? Spanish concessions to Basque autonomy and British efforts to guarantee a political role for the Catholics of Northern Ireland are, in part, reactions to terrorism. The social and political reforms implemented by the French during the Algerian war were similarly motivated by Front de Libération Nationale (FLN) terrorism, among other factors. In each case, however, reforms were accompanied by vigorous offensives against the terrorist organizations.

The international policy dimension is much more complex, depending on the cooperation of states who, while they may in common oppose terrorism, have divergent interests in other policy areas that affect the formulation and implementation of policies toward terrorism.[9] States disagree forcefully over what is terrorism and what is not. Thus cooperative efforts in international relations have focused, as has domestic law, on specific criminal actions such as hijackings and diplomatic kidnappings, which can be defined without ambiguity. Where international coordination, even with the best intentions,

9. Information on the international response can be found in Alona E. Evans and John F. Murphy, eds., *Legal Aspects of International Terrorism* (Lexington, Mass.: D. C. Heath, 1978). For action by the European community, see Juliet Lodge, ed., *Terrorism: A Challenge to the State* (New York: St. Martin's Press, 1981).

flounders is on the issue of the sovereign state's right to grant asylum to political offenders. The United States complains if Libya or Cuba grants political asylum but cannot guarantee extradition of IRA suspects to Great Britain. Attempts to provide automatic extradition or punishment of captured terrorists have consistently failed. In general, international policy has followed domestic policies in the trend toward "no concessions." In recent years the perception of terrorism as a common threat seems to have been strengthened rather than weakened. Thus, although multilateral treaties and agreements have not been as thorough, as comprehensive, or as strong as some states would prefer, the unilateral policies of states are often tacitly coordinated in recognition of a common interest.

Another point of change in foreign policy behavior that results directly from terrorism is the adoption of policies of forceful intervention against terrorist organizations on the territory of foreign states. Not only has Israel violated Lebanese sovereignty in attacking Palestinian strongholds, but both Israel and West Germany organized dramatic military expeditions to rescue hostages held by terrorists in third countries, which were willing or unwilling hosts. At the time of the Entebbe and Mogadishu incidents, there was concern over the precedent-setting nature of such unilateral use of force, which although defended as national "self-help" had an ambiguous status under international law. The tragic failure of the American rescue effort in Iran, however, demonstrated the difficulties of implementing such policies and probably discouraged imitation.

No policy toward terrorism is free of social and political costs. All policies toward terrorism can be analyzed in terms of negative side effects for civil liberties, not only in democratic states but in states where there is less freedom to be lost. Irving Louis Horowitz warns us of creeping infringements that are the more dangerous because they become normal to us; Robert Cox describes the extreme of thousands of "disappearances" Argentinian citizens not only denied could happen but denied did happen. There are also costs associated with inaction, costs that involve violations of the civil liberties of citizens by terrorists.

There are no general studies that document the concrete effects of policies against terrorism on individual freedoms. Therefore, we can only suggest tentatively that policies against terrorism do not seem to have seriously restricted civil liberties except where terrorism resulted in military dictatorship. For example, the authors of these essays agree that in West Germany, where terrorism was widely perceived as a crisis for democracy, the liberalism of the state has not been significantly weakened. In other Western democracies, controversial security measures have been short-lived. Opposition to the treatment of captured terrorist suspects in West Germany and Great Britain, for example, led to a halt in the objectionable practices, which included sensory deprivation techniques. The imposition of martial law as a response to FLQ terrorism in Quebec in 1970, a measure widely criticized at the time, did not apparently leave permanent scars. Fears of the transformation of Western democracies into garrison states therefore seem exaggerated, but we should be constantly alert to the consequences of terrorism for democratic practices.

Political attitudes and participation. It is difficult to evaluate the effects of terrorism on the political beliefs and behavior of individuals. We must consider not only the direct effects of terrorism but the consequences of terrorism's impact on power configurations, institutions, and public policies.

The effects of intimidation, of living in an atmosphere of constant danger and threat, are direct. In Northern Ireland, for example, trial by jury was made difficult if not impossible by IRA attacks on jurors. This development, which inhibited democratic participation, occasioned, at least in part, the introduction of the policy of internment without trial, which generated much controversy and sympathy for the IRA. The policy was subsequently abandoned, but only after significant damage to the British reputation. Similarly, prosecution of the Red Brigades in Italy has been hampered by assassinations of judges and prosecutors. In countries such as Algeria, El Salvador, or Guatemala, where rural terrorism accompanies extensive guerrilla warfare, voters are frequently intimidated. Threats and intimidation often reduce popular cooperation with the authorities. Attacks on public officials probably have a negative effect on recruitment into government positions. Recruitment into the diplomatic corps, especially the U.S. Foreign Service, may also be adversely affected by the risk of terrorism. In some countries, counterterrorism by or on behalf of the state also pressures citizens into supporting the regime and prevents the emergence of alternative leadership structures.

Moreover, terrorism polarizes the political attitudes of citizens regardless of personal threat. It is difficult for audiences to remain neutral; the more intense the terrorism, the more precarious the middle ground. When counterterrorism accompanies terrorism, neutrality is even more uncomfortable. Polarization is extreme in places like Northern Ireland, where terrorism reinforces preexisting historical, social, and religious cleavages. Ethnic or religious solidarity works in a similar fashion among Basques, Armenians, Puerto Ricans, and other groups with divided loyalties. Yet even where the lines are not already sharply drawn, terrorism poses fundamental political dilemmas of justice, obedience, and loyalty.

In cohesive societies or in states where terrorism is associated with a minority, terrorism usually increases majority support for the government. This has occurred in settings as disparate as West Germany, Argentina, and Israel. The fact that terrorism often intensifies support for the government even prompts Yehezkel Dror to the tongue-in-cheek suggestion that terrorism has practical advantages for governments in need of consolidating their support. Certainly the specter of revolution has been manipulated by right-wing governments and movements to gain power. Although threats and crises may deepen loyalty to the state and the order it is committed to preserving, the development of such solidarity in democracies works to discredit political dissent. All criticism of the regime may come to be linked in people's minds to terrorism and the advocacy of violence. Guilt by association—when opponents of the regime are accused of being terrorist "sympathizers"—is not an uncommon effect. The situation in West Germany, where intellectuals of the left were accused of sympathizing with terrorism when they criticized the government's restrictions on civil liberties, had a historical precedent in the 1890s and early 1900s in France and the United States, when anarchists were maligned and persecuted because of their association with terrorism, although the great majority of anarchists were peaceful in intent. Terrorism can in this fashion have a long-term effect on political values.

A vehement public reaction to terrorism may force the government to adopt policies against terrorism that independent decision-makers would consider unwise. Public pressure increases governments' propensity to act, a tendency already encouraged by the apparent simplicity of the immediate response. Responding to terrorism is much less complex, slow, and expensive than dealing with hunger, poverty, discrimination, or other intractable social problems. Terrorism frequently involves dramatic and emotional confrontations that attract publicity. The manner of the communication of the terrorist message in part determines perceptions of the content and influences the nature of the public reaction. Because the suspense and horror of terrorism make it instantly newsworthy, its importance as a threat to stability may be exaggerated. Public officials are acutely aware that an act of terrorism will precipitate a crowd of television reporters with cameras, waiting to broadcast the terms of the government's response.[10] Even if inaction—neither giving in nor intervening with force—should be the best choice, governments find it hard not to act. Thus the public reaction to terrorism may limit the government's options, encourage action either to offset an impression of

10. See Alex Schmid and Janny de Graaf, *Violence as Communication: Insurgent Terrorism and the Western News Media* (Beverly Hills: Sage, 1982). Ironically, the Israeli government has accused the Western press, not of exaggerating the role of terrorism but of minimizing it because correspondents have been intimidated by Palestinian terrorist organizations. See *New York Times*, February 14, 1982, p. 9.

weakness or resolve the crisis at high cost, and increase the cost of not acting.

Prospects of future violence. Terrorism may increase or decrease the likelihood of continued or expanded violence. Three basic questions need to be considered: Does terrorism stimulate more terrorism, whether by the same organization, by "second-generation" groups, or by imitators in other countries? Does terrorism result in violence by the state or by elements acting in its name? Does terrorism lead directly or indirectly to broader violence, with widened popular involvement?

Terrorism is demonstrably a contagious phenomenon.[11] Its roots in various national contexts are not completely indigenous; events in one country may inspire imitation in others.

Terrorist organizations frequently have direct, physical contacts with other terrorist groups and with foreign countries. Collaboration extends to buying weapons, finding asylum, obtaining passports and false documents, acquiring funds, and sometimes rendering assistance in the planning and execution of terrorist attacks. For example, Western European terrorists have been known to train at Palestinian camps. The Italian Red Brigade has links with the West German terrorists and Czechoslovakia. The IRA has received assistance from Libya. The Japanese Red Army participated with Palestinians in attacks on Israel. The existence of such a terrorist network does not in itself imply the existence of a centrally directed conspiracy, but it does mean that transnational links among groups with shared aims make terrorism in one state likely to lead to terrorism in nearby states.

In addition, the contagion process may operate in the absence of physical contacts when terrorist organizations, often geographically distant, become significant models for imitation. The Tupamaros of Uruguay became a compelling model for terrorism in West Germany and Italy. Propitious circumstances in

11. For an analysis of the contagion effects of terrorism, see Manus I. Midlarsky, Martha Crenshaw, and Fumihiko Yoshida, "Why Violence Spreads: The Contagion of International Terrorism," *International Studies Quarterly* 24 (June 1980): 262–98.

Western Europe—the 1968 student revolt, anti-Americanism, and general disillusionment with capitalism and democracy—enhanced the receptivity of some dissidents to the model of a Third World revolutionary group combating American imperialism. The romantic and moral appeal of the Tupamaros was well-publicized and articulated in ideological terms compatible with the beliefs of West European radicals. West European left extremists and Tupamaros resembled each other as well in their well-educated, middle-class backgrounds. Moreover, terrorism is a highly imitable innovation in violent tactics; it combines drama, symbolism, low cost, and ease of implementation. It is also admirably adapted to the urban environment. Thus powerful models can stimulate the imitation of terrorism in the absence of direct communications.

Terrorism may produce further violence in a context of fragmented power. An uncontrolled response, whether public or private, often degenerates into a destructive cycle of terrorism and counterterrorism. Examples can be found in Argentina, Northern Ireland, Turkey, and Algeria. Vengeance and irrationality can come to motivate both sides of the struggle. Robert Cox argues that in Argentina, the counterterrorism of the security forces was a consequence of frustration over their own ineptitude in combating terrorism. An inefficient police and military combined with a weak or complacent central government encourages both counterterrorism and terrorism.

Yet it must be recognized that a real dilemma confronts the policy-makers even of stable, centralized regimes. Any use of force, short of the lengths of repression to which democracies are unwilling to go, is unlikely to halt terrorism in the short run and indeed is likely to encourage it. But not taking the offensive against terrorism also carries risks. Inaction allows the terrorists free rein, damages the government's reputation, and opens the door to exasperated private retaliation.

Thus popular pressure, fear of loss of control, and the challenge of violence make a response of moderate coercion the only practical choice for most democratic regimes. A terrorist campaign once launched seems to persist for an initial period because of its internal dynamics. That is, under the best of circumstances, security forces can only gradually penetrate and dismantle a terrorist conspiracy that is prepared in advance and committed to action. During this critical initial period, what governments can do is avoid actions that give added impetus to terrorism or enlarge the sphere of violence.

A government may inadvertently add to its troubles by an inconsistent response. Government policies that alternate between unusual severity and leniency, perhaps as a result of reacting in haste to the immediate crisis and then relaxing in the aftermath, are likely to provoke terrorism. A strong show of force against a background of moderation or relative tolerance appears unfair and unjust to terrorists, who are sensitive to appearances of injustice. Not only are expectations violated, but a case for vengeance, one of the strongest motives for terrorism, is established. Solidarity with one's comrades is an equally powerful incentive. Policy-makers are therefore confronted with another choice between bad and worse: terrorists killed by police or executed by the state become useful "martyrs" to the cause, but imprisoned terrorists stimulate their comrades to attempt to free them through further terrorism. The government is put on the defensive in either situation.

Governments may fail to limit punitive measures to the appropriate target. In the initial stage of terrorism, it is difficult to acquire useful information about the conspiracy. Ignorant of who the terrorists are—and they are typically a small number—the government is tempted to arrest the opponents it knows and to arrest indiscriminately. Suspects from familiar opposition movements are arrested, interrogated, even held in preventive detention. Few of those caught off guard are terrorists (who are the only ones prepared for repression). The net effect is to promote recruitment into the terrorist organization. British internment centers in Northern Ireland were frequently dubbed ideal recruiting camps for the IRA. Prisoners who were not members when they went in were when they came out. Where the terrorist organization is affiliated with a particular ethnic or religious community, government arrests and interrogations risk appearing discriminatory and unfair, increasing distrust of the government and sympathy for the terrorists, a polarization particularly evident in Northern Ireland and on the West Bank under Israeli rule.

Finally, the contradictory effects of terrorism on political culture—on popular traditions, values, and beliefs—could gradually create propitious circumstances for violence. The routinization of terrorism Irving Louis Horowitz fears could slowly transform standards of acceptable political expression. Exposure to terrorism may increase public tolerance to the point that terrorism becomes normal, or at least usual and ordinary. Some authors claim that the attention given the phenomenon by scholars and policy-makers works to make terrorism commonplace. David Apter believes that "learning to live with terrorism will make it as ordinary as crime or poverty or undisposed garbage. Analysis of terrorism is its own form of social restoration."[12] Furthermore, if the premise is correct that the most important determinant of the policy response to terrorism is public opinion, then terrorists may escalate their actions in order to shock an apathetic or numbed public consciousness, leading to the expansion of terrorism that Yehezkel Dror outlines in his essay.

On the other hand, public attitudes may develop in a way that equates all radicalism with terrorism and discredits critics of the established order as "terrorist sympathizers." Intolerance for dissent could lead to wider violence if avenues of peaceful political change were closed, on the international as well as the national level. Ironically, terrorism could strengthen conservative political forces to such a degree that the revolution conservatives most fear would become a self-fulfilling prophecy. Provoking the state into creating revolutionary conditions is in fact the aim of some terrorists.[13]

12. David E. Apter, "Notes on the Underground: Left Violence and the National State," *Daedalus* 108 (Fall 1979): 167.
13. Carlos Marighela, for example, explains that the aim of revolutionary strategy is to "oblige the enemy to transform the country's political situation into a military one. Then discontent will spread to all social groups and the

Neither of these two changes in political culture is likely to be rapid. The general stability of political attitudes works in favor of a continuation of moderate views. But these transformations could in time lead to a sharp division of attitudes both within Western democracies and worldwide.

Social Effects

The social, like the political, consequences of terrorism vary greatly according to the intensity of the terrorist campaign. It is hard to compare American society, largely untouched by terrorism, to that of Northern Ireland. Terrorism is but one source of social tensions and in comparison to other problems much less important, but it has a sharp impact in small societies where much of the population is affected and in homogeneous societies whose members often identify closely with the victims.

When we speak of the social effects of terrorism, we are thinking not of systemic changes in social structure but of smaller, incremental changes, primarily in attitudes of trust and in social cohesion and integration. Little comparative research has been done on this problem, although there are case studies of the extremes like Northern Ireland.[14] We should also be careful to remember that the results of terrorism are not always negative; it may perform some positive social functions, for instance, in creating or maintaining social solidarity.[15]

What immediately strikes the observer of the social consequences of terrorism is the extraordinary resilience and strength of the social order. Even in the most acutely disturbed societies, life goes on with superficial normality. People adjust to conditions that from an outsider's point of view are intolerable. This is not to say that the social effects of terrorism can be dismissed but that society survives violent stress. As Horowitz

---

military will be held exclusively responsible for failures" (*For the Liberation of Brazil* [Harmondsworth: Penguin, 1971], p. 46).

14. A controversial example is Rona M. Fields, *Northern Ireland: Society under Siege* (New Brunswick: Transaction Books, 1980; a reprint of the 1977 edition published by Temple University Press).

15. Lewis A. Coser, *The Functions of Social Conflict* (New York: Free Press, 1956).

argues, terrorism is more likely to become a fact of life than a continual source of shock.[16]

Despite the enduring stability of the social order, a noticeable result of terrorism by one social or ethnic group against another—as the IRA against Protestants, Algerians against European settlers, or Palestinians against Israelis—is the reinforcement of group boundaries, increased cohesion within each community, and the widening of the gap between groups. Terrorism seems to reinforce tendencies to stereotype the outgroup as the enemy. These changes in turn affect living and employment patterns, as territorial boundaries of communities become sharply delineated. There are areas of Belfast and Beirut, for example, where only members of the resident community feel safe.

Furthermore, it is difficult to estimate the long-term effect on social relationships of living under conditions of uncertainty, danger, fear, suspicion, and hatred. Inhabitants of societies like Northern Ireland, where a subculture of violence exists on both sides, surely experience consequences that severely damage political socialization. Lack of communication and trust inhibits political compromise and accommodation. Terrorism isolates communities and breeds ignorance and suspicion. An added consequence in Northern Ireland is a high level of emigration.

In less bitterly affected societies, the slight effects of terrorism may eventually add up to a heavy burden. For example, terrorism results in a decrease in social interchanges because of physical dangers. Tourism to threatened areas fall off. There are substantial lifestyle changes for foreign business executives sent to high-risk countries; risk-analysis firms are employed to estimate precisely what the dangers are. These changes, although they affect small numbers of people, inhibit openness, decrease communication, destroy confidence, and invade privacy.

16. In this respect, it would be interesting to compare the effects of terrorism with those of crime.

Heinrich Böll's most recent novel, *The Safety Net*, describes the social consequences of adapting to terrorism in contemporary West Germany.[17] Life under the shadow of terrorism imposes galling constraints on the choices of the wealthy and the prominent, whose decisions in matters of houses, schools, shopping, and travel are dictated by security considerations. They are victims of their protectors, who monitor all conversations, visitors, and movement. The victims develop distorted perceptions of the world: all objects and situations come to be defined in terms of where bombs could be disguised, kidnappers concealed, or assassins posted. Furthermore, the loss of privacy, freedom, and spontaneity is not restricted to the potential victims of terrorism; neighbors and acquaintances must also, to their annoyance, share the penalties of surveillance. Number of bodyguards replaces number of servants as a mark of social status. Terrorism also leads to a deepening isolation of former student rebels, who are socially ostracized, unemployable, and the targets of official suspicion. Although they have repudiated violence, they constitute a generation without a place in society. Böll's work also reveals the peculiar intimacy of terrorism in West Germany, a society in which terrorists, victims, and misfits may be members of the same family.

The social consequences of terrorism have a direct bearing on political outcomes. Acclimation to terrorism, to diminished trust in social relationships, to instability of expectations with regard to behavior, and to loss of personal privacy without a corresponding gain in security risks discrediting the social foundations of the liberal state. If the social underpinnings of democracy are destroyed while the state's ability to maintain order is weakened, then democratic governments may indeed become fragile. David Apter fears that in such a social and po-

17. Trans. Leila Vennewitz (New York: Alfred A. Knopf, 1982). Originally published as *Fürsorgliche Belagerung* (Cologne: Verlag Kiepenheuer & Witsch, 1979). Reviewer Robert Alter emphasizes Böll's perception of terrorism "not as a dangerous disease which might possibly be avoided by stringent political hygiene, but as a permanent, established symptom of our malaise and our impotence, a symptom the patient is learning to live with willy-nilly" (*The New Republic*, March 3, 1982, p. 31).

litical environment, terrorist organizations are likely to gain clients:

> The success of terrorism thus needs to be measured by the impotency of government, but also in the degree that people withdraw from society, retreat from civility, and avoid public space, to live instead with alarm systems, dogs, and guns, all instruments of a society where every man is for himself, a hermetic society, a society without trust or obligation—a condition under which cell life prospers.[18]

An intriguing sidelight on the social consequences of terrorism concerns the role of women. There has been considerable speculation about the prominent position of women in terrorist groups (not prominent in comparison to the number of women in the population at large but in proportion to the number of women active in politics or in leadership roles).[19] It will be interesting to find out if female participation in violence will have an effect on general social roles or on the stereotyping of women.

The Effectiveness of Terrorism

Beyond classifying and weighing the political and social consequences of terrorism lies the problem of assessing its effectiveness as an instrument of political change. Do the results of terrorism represent its success or failure? Can we explain why and when terrorism is effective?

It is necessary to evaluate the effectiveness of terrorism in two different perspectives. First, does terrorism succeed in obtaining the goals the terrorists set for themselves? Answering this question requires careful analysis of terrorist goals on a case-by-case basis. Fortunately, the literature on the aims of terrorist organizations is substantial.[20]

18. "Notes on the Underground," p. 169.
19. Jane Alpert, *Growing up Underground* (New York: William Morrow, 1981), provides an account of her experiences in the Weather Underground. Another memoir by a female terrorist is Leila Khaled, *My People Shall Live: The Autobiography of a Revolutionary* (London: Hodder and Stoughton, 1973).
20. For an early article on the subject, see Thomas P. Thornton, "Terror as a Weapon of Political Agitation," in Harry Eckstein, ed., *Internal War: Problems*

The second problem is to analyze terrorism's capacity for causing significant political change, regardless of whether such change is intended by the terrorist organization. In considering unanticipated as well as anticipated consequences, we wish to know why in some cases and not in others terrorism has undermined democratic principles or seriously threatened political order and stability, even if such changes were not the desired outcome of the terrorist organization.

All terrorist organizations, whether the long-term political outcome they seek is revolution, national self-determination, preservation or restoration of the status quo, or reform, are engaged in a struggle for political power with a government they wish to influence or replace. The analysis of the effects of terrorism on domestic power relationships demonstrates that terrorism as a grand strategy of overthrowing regimes is an illusion; however, most terrorists act according to long-term strategies and may consider partial movement toward their goals as success. Therefore any increase, however limited, in the terrorist organization's influence over the political process is meaningful.

The position from which the terrorist organization seeks to increase its power is one of extreme weakness in coercive capabilities. The government cannot be challenged militarily on the level of physical force. Thus, as Conor Cruise O'Brien maintains, the power of terrorism is through political legitimacy, winning acceptance in the eyes of a significant population and discrediting the government's legitimacy. The terrorist organization challenges the regime's right to possess a monopoly of force in society and physically demonstrates its inability to maintain order. The resources potentially available to serious terrorist groups, those with long-run ideological ambitions to change the political order, thus lie largely in public perceptions.

---

and Approaches (New York: Free Press, 1964), pp. 71–99. Nathan Leites has provided an interesting analysis of how terrorists in developed countries make their calculations plausible to themselves in terms of their stated goals: "Understanding the Next Act," *Terrorism: An International Journal* 3 (1979): 1–46. See also Paul Wilkinson, *Political Terrorism* (New York: Wiley, 1974).

Under what conditions, then, do terrorists succeed in acquiring relative political power, instrumental to producing the outcomes they seek or to causing significant change? Several factors are useful in explaining the political results of terrorism: properties of the terrorist group, including size, organization, leadership, intensity of commitment, techniques of violence, and goals; characteristics of both the domestic and the international situation, including the role of the press, political culture, and social structure; and the governmental response, considered as an asset or an obstacle to terrorism's effectiveness.

The Terrorist Organization

Other things being equal, tightly organized, disciplined, skilled, well-led terrorist organizations are most efficient and successful in tactical terms. Groups with foreign links often have access to resources that parochial groups do not. Nationalist and revolutionary groups possess stronger commitment and tend to be more thoroughly organized than reactionary groups. Size is the least significant attribute: a handful of terrorists can create mayhem in a modern, technology-dependent society.

The practical abilities of terrorist groups also play a role in determining the initiation and the outcome of bargaining terrorism. When in the late 1960s seizing hostages for ransom was a new development, terrorist organizations could reasonably expect many governments to meet their demands. At present, terrorists seem more likely to seize hostages not to compel compliance with specific demands, such as the release of prisoners, but to gain recognition and to demonstrate political power. Their aim is to retain mastery of the situation and to appear victorious at the end, to gain a better power position for the next round.[21] In the absence of government concessions, terrorist superiority means releasing or murdering the hostage while escaping unpunished. Success thus requires meticulous

---

21. See Jeanne H. Knutson, "The Terrorists' Dilemmas: Some Implicit Rules of the Game," *Terrorism: An International Journal* 4 (1980): 195–222.

preparation, the possession of a secure home base, intense commitment, and willingness to take high risks. Only the more efficient groups, operating on familiar ground, can expect to succeed.

Tactical success strongly depends on the organizational strengths of a terrorist group; strategic success over the long term seems to be closely linked to the organization's goal. Only when the potential exists for a sympathetic reaction from a politically influential audience will a terrorist organization gain legitimacy. Legitimacy requires recognition by a significant public, and ideally by government decision-makers as well, of the *salience* and the *justice* of the terrorists' cause. What the terrorists want must be seen as both important and right.

The reactions of three types of audience are instrumental in the achievement of terrorist goals. They are distinguished by degree of receptivity to the terrorist message (admittedly, their existence and predispositions are in a sense situational factors over which the terrorists have no control): (1) An audience may be predisposed toward sympathy for the terrorists' aims, as for example, national or ethnic groups to calls for national liberation or secession. In this case, terrorism can be effective in mobilizing enthusiasm and active support. A terrorist organization may profit by being the extremist faction of a broader social movement; examples include the Basque Euzkadi ta Askatasuna (ETA) or the Irgun in Mandate Palestine. (2) An audience may be indifferent to or ignorant of the terrorists' appeal, in which case terrorism may gain recognition for the claims the terrorists represent and may also attract sympathy and support for a hitherto unknown cause. The metropolitan populations of colonial countries fell into this category. Terrorism apparently helped convince the populations of Great Britain and France that maintaining an unruly colony was an intolerable burden. (3) An audience may be predisposed to hostility to the terrorists' aims, as for example, religious, ethnic, or nationalist rivals for control of the same territory. In this case, terrorism can only increase intransigence and opposition. For example, terrorism is unlikely to compel Northern Irish Protestants to agree to IRA demands.

The Palestinian case illustrates these distinctions. Terrorism against Israel has only heightened Israeli loyalty to the state and determination to resist Palestinian nationalist demands. The Israeli population is not frightened into submission by terrorism. Terrorist activity, however, by dramatizing the Palestinian cause and the commitment of militant groups to righting political grievances, aroused latent nationalism in a disheartened Palestinian diaspora, gained the active political and sometimes military assistance of Arab regimes and peoples, and jarred the previously unconcerned and neutral international community into an awareness of Palestinian nationalism that has grown increasingly sympathetic. The Palestinian goal of national self-determination is one extended audiences worldwide are likely to perceive as legitimate. As Eugene V. Walter has argued about a different case, for terrorism to be effective in enhancing the power of the terrorist group, its ideological justification must be one an audience can share.[22] The ends to which terrorism is put must be viewed as morally justified.

Furthermore, for terrorism to appear legitimate there must be a congruence between ends and means; both the resort to terrorism and the particular form it takes should seem appropriate to the cause at hand. (Inappropriateness of means to ends may explain why terrorism is rarely a technique of political protest, as opposed to a technique of revolution or national liberation.) For instance, selective terrorism against specific agents of the regime is more likely to be effective because its meaning is clear and it can be justified on moral grounds. Terrorism that sharpens and simplifies distinctions between friends and enemies is more likely to be approved by potential friends. Terrorism is less effective when it confuses the audi-

---

22. *Terror and Resistance: A Study of Political Violence* (New York: Oxford University Press, 1969), pp. 340–41. Walter explains that "legitimacy suppresses outrage."

ence's loyalties. Indiscriminate terrorism resulting in large numbers of anonymous casualties may initially attract greater publicity, but over the long run it even becomes less newsworthy. Terrorists with little chance of developing a constituency may sacrifice legitimacy and consequently long-term effectiveness for the instant gain of notoriety, but it is a gain that quickly dissipates.

The relative capabilities of terrorist organizations affect the choice of method. Only the better organized and more resourceful organizations have the resources to pinpoint targets. Bombings of anonymous victims are much easier than assassinations of well-guarded leaders.

Ideology also makes a large difference, when it dictates forms and targets. Modern revolutionary-socialist terrorists self-consciously strike at capitalists and imperialists; to choose working-class victims would be contrary to the tenets of their beliefs. On the other hand, the philosophical convictions of fascist or neofascist terrorists include mythic affirmations of the value and necessity of violence for its own sake.[23] Thus extremists of the right, who are also often less rigorously organized and disciplined than the more rationalistic left, are frequently responsible for indiscriminately destructive acts such as the bombing at the Bologna railroad station in August 1980, whereas the self-styled heirs of Marx and Lenin, such as the Revolutionary Cells in West Germany, aim at symbols of the American military presence.

The Structure of the Situation

The domestic and international contexts in which terrorism occurs are also important, especially when they increase the probability of popular support.

A free press to report terrorist exploits is essential for communicating the terrorist appeal to wide audiences. The mode and tone of reporting can obviously influence the reception of

23. See Thomas Sheehan, "Myth and Violence: The Fascism of Julius Evola and Alain de Benoist," *Social Research* 48 (Spring 1981): 45–73.

the message. Since publicity is a result that terrorists operating in democracies can count on, censorship of the press might diminish terrorism's effectiveness in the short run. Not only would restrictions on freedom of the press be the sort of Faustian bargain that Irving Louis Horowitz deplores, but it would be impossible to stop the flow of all information about terrorism. Furthermore, Robert Cox observes that in authoritarian regimes, where self-censorship often makes officially imposed restrictions unnecessary, neither mode of social control can be guaranteed to inhibit terrorism.

Historical traditions, myths, and symbols determine the outcomes of terrorist campaigns. As Conor Cruise O'Brien emphasizes, in Ireland, North and South, the long history of British oppression legitimizes Provisional IRA terrorism despite the reality of essential differences between the martyrs of 1916 and the Provisional IRA. The fascist pasts of West Germany, Italy, and Japan have been significant both in motivating terrorism and in shaping the domestic and international reaction.

Social structure influences outcomes by molding audience predispositions. Careful distinctions must be made among terrorist activities directed from within homogeneous societies, externally directed against homogeneous societies, or led by factions in societies divided by ethnic or religious cleavages. West Germany, Israel, and Northern Ireland are instructive cases. In West Germany, terrorism has resulted in noticeable institutional and policy changes, which have not, in the opinion of the symposium authors, damaged the fundamental commitment to democracy. The majority of the republic rallied strongly to its defense while refusing to sanction repressive measures or a resurgence of right-wing extremism. Yet the issue of loyalty to the state became central to political life, and self-doubt and anxiety, particularly about the lessons of Germany's past, have grown. For terrorism to come from the sons and daughters of the ruling elite is a distressing phenomenon for Western democracies, as we have seen in the United States, West Germany, Italy, and Japan. In Israel, however, where the enemy is a stranger, it simply reinforced solidarity and the determination to resist. In Northern Ireland, two national communities are trapped in the same state, which neither now rules. The proximity and intimacy of neighbors only increase bitterness and hatred. Neither community can seal off its borders although each can identify the enemy by schooling, accent, home, and religion. The stalemate that results from the inability of either side to win only widens the divisions.

Other social factors such as patterns of prejudice and discrimination are also significant. The discrimination Catholics endured at the hands of British and Protestants legitimizes the cause of the IRA. Israeli attitudes toward Palestinians are partly determined by the perception of Arabs as socially inferior. Long-standing prejudices make it easier to stereotype the other side as the enemy and to justify one's own righteousness.

Government Response

The actions of terrorist organizations and the context they act in are important to the outcomes of campaigns of terrorism against the state, but the actions or nonactions of government policy-makers are equally critical to the effectiveness of terrorism.[24] The accomplishments of terrorists are by no means automatic; the government response can be either an obstacle or an asset to success. As in our analysis of the choices of the terrorist organization, we are dealing here with the political decisions of government elites. These decisions are constrained by the terrorists' initiatives and by the social, economic, and political "givens" of the situation, which neither of the major actors—terrorists or government—controls. Yet governments have choices in how to combat terrorism—choices that can be key determinants of the outcome.

As Anthony Quainton argues, the essence of the govern-

24. The argument that government response is important to outcomes is supported by the work of Juan J. Linz and others on how and why democratic regimes break down. In analyzing the political dynamics of breakdown, Linz emphasizes how the behavior of the incumbents when confronted by crisis contributes to the demise of the regime (*Crisis, Breakdown, and Reequilibration*, published as a separate introductory volume in the paperback edition of Juan J. Linz and Alfred Stepan, eds., *The Breakdown of Democratic Regimes* [Baltimore: Johns Hopkins University Press, 1978]).

ment's problem is to maintain and strengthen its authority while diminishing the legitimacy of the terrorists. Thus the government faced with terrorism must be concerned with both the effectiveness and the legitimacy of its policies.[25] At the outset a significant difference exists between states whose authority is secure—whether because of strong coercive power or the long-term legitimacy of the institutions of the state and the socioeconomic order it defends—and those whose authority is weak. The analysis of terrorism's effects on the distribution of political power within states suggests that only those regimes that are already unstable are vulnerable to break down under the pressure of terrorism. In democratic states as well, as Yehezkel Dror explains, terrorism must be seen as part of a larger and more complex problem of the capacity to govern.

Thus it is not necessarily irrelevant, as Yehezkel Dror contends, for democratic governments to attempt to deal with the sources of terrorism. Left-revolutionary terrorism against the democratic state often poses a fundamental problem. Can the regime defend and preserve the legitimacy of the basic political values, institutions, and procedures of the state while admitting the existence of the need for reform in both the political system and the socioeconomic order? Is reform, such as autonomy for the Basque region of Spain, an admission of the justice of terrorist claims and, furthermore, of the right to use violence in support of those claims? It is important that the government make a clear distinction between the ends and the means of terrorism; ironically, the means of terrorism cannot be allowed to discredit the ends. The eradication of what appear to be the sources of terrorism—discrimination or deprivation—is not certain to prevent terrorism, but it may decrease its potential for legitimacy.

For example, what legitimacy the Red Brigade possesses (undoubtedly small, but a quality which is impossible to measure) is surely attributable to the Italian government's corruption, general inefficiency, and inability to solve persistent social and

25. Linz discusses the distinction between efficacy and effectiveness and the relationship between effectiveness and legitimacy (*Crisis*, pp. 16–23).

economic problems.[26] Terrorism in Italy has highlighted the need for prisoner reform, for improved conditions for workers in the North, and for an end to poverty and underdevelopment in the South, as well as the government's incompetence. Terrorism exposed, but did not create, serious problems. It also vividly demonstrated that the government could not assure the personal security of its employees, of social and economic elites, or of foreign dignitaries. Yet the majority of the population continues to support the state, not only out of loyalty but from the habit of obedience, the fear of sanctions, and the anticipation of material rewards—none of which the terrorist organization can realistically offer. Moreover, the political alternative the terrorists present is unpalatable to the majority. As long as terrorism does not result in substantial popular mobilization against the state, the government will not fall to revolution from the left. There is, however, a risk of counterrevolution, of a military coup d'etat or a takeover from the right. (Such a consequence has also been greatly feared in Spain, as a result of Basque terrorism.)

If the government is to issue a credible denial of terrorist claims that the existing socioeconomic order and the institutions of the state are unjust, its position and policies must be above reproach. The argument that combating terrorism requires using terrorist methods is not only morally abhorrent but politically disastrous. Actions against the terrorists must be scrupulously legal. Governments must also maintain effective control over the response to terrorism. Delegations of authority to autonomous security bureaucracies or to private organizations undermine the state's legitimacy. Both the history of the results of terrorism and the analysis of its relationship to the legitimacy of regimes support the proposition that tolerating a right-wing counterterrorist reaction, especially the formation of private paramilitary units or vigilantes, is destabilizing. Therefore, governments must often resist popular pressures for immediate action. Defeating ongoing campaigns

26. For analysis of the Italian case, see the special issue, "Terrorism in Italy," of *Terrorism: An International Journal* 2, nos. 3 & 4 (1979).

of terrorism takes time; it is more important to avoid broadening the popular base of participation in violence than to commit the state to a hasty, overly strong response.

The policy response discussed thus far has concerned terrorism as a direct threat to the domestic security of the state and as a struggle for influence over the same population. Terrorism is also a foreign policy problem, particularly for the United States, a prime target of terrorism outside its borders. Terrorism is a transnational phenomenon, rarely contained within a single nation-state; attempts to combat it have clearly revealed the interdependence of states in the international order. Nevertheless, the differential impact of terrorism on world order has prevented the development of anything more than rudimentary international coping mechanisms directed specifically against hijackings and diplomatic kidnappings. Although the most efficient policies are unilateral or bilateral, there is an important and little noticed factor, which Anthony Quainton mentions. On the international scene, terrorism has become substantially delegitimized. It has become less rather than more acceptable as a means of bringing about change in the international order. Research is needed to discover why the international result of terrorism is apparently a reinforcement of the community of states, despite the notoriety of nations such as Iran and Libya that use or condone terrorism as an instrument of foreign policy.

The existence of such "crazy states," to borrow a term coined by Yehezkel Dror in another context,[27] is an important issue for the United States. The practical difficulty for the victim of this oblique form of warfare lies in establishing the guilt of the instigator and in finding an appropriate mode of retaliation. This problem has no easy solution, but governments should remember that the issue at stake is international legitimacy, not the possession of superior force. Governments resorting to terrorism have received very little support from other states.

Another foreign policy problem concerns diplomatic, eco-

27. Yehezkel Dror, *Crazy States: A Counterconventional Strategic Problem* 2d ed. (Milwood, N.Y.: Kraus Reprint, 1980).

nomic, and military support for regimes whose response to internal violence from the left is repressive or counterterrorist force, involving persistent violations of civil rights. It is difficult to see how the interest of the United States in defending democracy and international order can benefit by pretending that unstable regimes, weak in legitimacy, are incipient democracies, even if they should be important to the global balance of power. There is a fundamental contradiction in condemning the practices of one's enemies and excusing those of one's friends. Terrorism is a unitary phenomenon, occurring in varied political contexts. The term should not be used as a political weapon.

A last question with respect to the government's response concerns the general effectiveness of democracies in combating terrorism. Is democracy a liability in the struggle? It is difficult to ascertain whether or not terrorism has been significantly prevented by the policies pursued by democratic states. We cannot explain why terrorism does not happen; only when it does do we attempt to discover what went wrong. Yehezkel Dror points to an "equifinality" of outcomes of government policies as a complicating factor. Governments usually claim a victory whatever the concrete result of an act of terrorism. If it ends with a negotiated solution, the government takes credit for saving the lives of the hostages. If it ends in bloodshed, the government claims that holding to a firm line has deterred future terrorism. Some observers may disagree with this rationale, noting, for example, the difference between the death of Aldo Moro and the rescue of General James L. Dozier in their relative consequences for the reputation of the Italian government. The image of failure incurs a high political cost. Thus an emphasis on the importance of legitimacy in combating terrorism and reducing its effectiveness does not obviate the need for efficient policy. Efficiency and legitimacy, as Robert Cox suggests, are closely related.

Terrorism is a pervasive source of disorder, with, however, a very uneven impact on political stability and social order. Although only marginally disruptive to international relations, it has affected the internal order of some states deeply and others lightly, in a pattern that is difficult to discern. The critical factor in accounting for terrorism's effect may be the ability of the terrorist organization to become a legitimate political force within a state. As often as not, government actions more than terrorism itself undermine the authority of the state. In particular, we concluded, on the basis of several of the essays in this volume, that a complacent dismissal of the experiences of Argentina and Northern Ireland as exceptions and as irrelevant to the concerns of "normal" politics would be unwise.

Terrorism evokes an extraordinary and emotional concern in democratic states, not only because their leaders and citizens feel threatened and are shocked to find that currents of political disaffection can run so deep but because of the widespread awareness that the response to terrorism can imperil democratic values. Yet when we scrutinize closely the effects both of terrorism and of the policies employed to combat it, we see that terrorism has not so far been responsible for the breakdown of democratic regimes. The free press, often perceived as a liability in the struggle against terrorism, provides only short-term publicity, which quickly recedes if the cause the terrorists claim to represent is not central to the public's political interests. Publicity alone does not determine effectiveness.

Although there are cures for terrorism that are undoubtedly worse than the disease, one need not despair of all remedies. Democracies have in general proved resilient, even if we do not fully understand the conditions that promote good health. Terrorism is only one of the growing number of social and political problems that modern governments cannot solve, yet the nation-state shows remarkable tenacity and remains the primary symbol of political legitimacy, the focus of popular loyalties, and the basis of international order.

It appears that unstable regimes of mixed character, neither democratic nor rigidly authoritarian, are most vulnerable to changes in the locus of political power. Uruguay is the most democratic of the regimes that have fallen under the impact of terrorism, but our knowledge of the end of civilian rule in Uruguay is insufficient to permit generalization to other cases. Thus we should look carefully and critically not only at the democracies where terrorists have been alarmingly active but at fragile mixed regimes that can be tipped to counterterrorism and repression by terrorism. Terrorism could shift certain of these regimes further away from democracy. We should be concerned about the preservation of democratic values even in settings where they are limited.

People who live in societies largely free of terrorism find it difficult to imagine the insecurity terrorism can create in different circumstances. It is to be hoped that the collection of sober, reflective, and well-informed essays in this volume will dispel both ignorance and misunderstanding of the nature of the problem of terrorism. They emphasize the need to recognize and respond to the consequences of terrorism without exaggerating its effectiveness. By avoiding sensationalism, by clarifying moral judgments, and by airing controversies, these analyses significantly further the neglected study of the results of terrorism.

Irving Louis Horowitz

2

The Routinization of Terrorism and Its Unanticipated Consequences

A subtle and far-ranging shift has occurred in the grammar of politics. In the 1970s congressional committees studied "alleged assassination plots involving foreign leaders" in which Senator Frank Church's Select Committee to Study Government Operations bluntly accused the executive branch of the United States of "institutionalizing assassination" through CIA actions.[1] In the 1980s congressional committees emphasize problems of "security and terrorism," and Senator Jeremiah Denton's equally select subcommittee on Security and Terrorism of the committee on the Judiciary takes up issues ranging from the origin, direction, and support of terrorism to the Turkish experience with terrorism.[2] Undergirding this shift

1. See U.S., Congress, Senate, Select Committee to Study Government Operations with Respect to Intelligence Activities, *Alleged Assassination Plots Involving Foreign Leaders: Interim Report*, 94th Cong., 1st Sess., Nov. 20, 1975.

2. See U.S., Congress, Senate, Committee on the Judiciary, Subcommittee on Security and Terrorism, *Terrorism: Origins, Direction and Support: Hearing*, 97th Cong., 1st Sess., April 24, 1981; *Intelligence Identities Protection Act of 1981: Hearing on S. 391*, 97th Cong., 1st Sess., May 8, 1981; *Historical Antecedents of Soviet Terrorism: Hearings*, 97th Cong., 1st Sess., June 11 and 12, 1981; *Terrorism: The Turkish Experience: Hearing*, 97th Cong., 1st Sess., June 25, 1981; *Terrorism: The Role of Moscow and Its Subcontractors: Hearing*, 97th Cong., 1st Sess., June 26, 1981.

in the rhetoric of committee reports is a profound transformation in the public sense of where the main danger to American society resides—not in internal police power but in external guerrilla power. The question of terrorism, far from being a simple academic exercise, is front and center in the political stage. A review of current policy with respect to terrorism is clearly in order.

In the last decade terrorism has become routine. The number of incidents of international terrorism, which has the support of a foreign government or organization or is directed against foreign persons or interests, almost doubled in the decade 1970–80. Deaths resulting from international terrorism in the same period increased from 131 to 642; terrorist attacks causing casualties (especially bombings and assassinations) have risen dramatically.[3] Once extraordinary and unusual phenomena have become normal, everyday events. Analyzing acts of terror has become a major activity for an enlarged intelligence industry. Nevertheless, we have not thought much about the social and political consequences of the routinization of terror. Social scientists and historians have made exhaustive analyses of everything from the causes of terrorism, to the nature of the terrorist, to the relationship of terrorism to ideology. But what are the consequences of terrorism—unanticipated and otherwise?

The literature of the causes of terrorism is rich.[4] If the causes of terrorism can be established and eradicated, then study of its consequences becomes moot. But we are no closer to determining terrorism's roots and eradicating them than we were ten

3. The best single source on the geographic distribution, category of attack, and number of casualties caused by terrorism is contained in National Foreign Assessment Center, *Patterns of International Terrorism: 1980* (Washington: National Technical Information Service, 1981). This report is also available in *Defense and Economy World Report and Survey*, July 20, 1981, pp. 46–57. Additional information is contained in "A New Surge of Terrorism" in *U.S. News and World Report*, Sept. 14, 1981; and James Berry Motley, "International Terrorism: A New Mode of Warfare," *International Security Review* 6 (Spring 1981): 93–123.

4. See Martha Crenshaw, "The Causes of Terrorism," *Comparative Politics* 13 (July 1981): 379–99; and Paul Wilkinson, *Terrorism and the Liberal State* (New York: Wiley, 1977); James Q. Wilson, "The Terrorist's Goal Is *Not* to Solve the Problem," *Washington Star*, July 19, 1981, sec. F, p. 1.

years ago. If terrorism is to remain very much a living presence in our midst, we had best be more deeply appreciative of its limitations as well as its potentials.

Those who have examined the consequences of terrorism can be grouped into two general camps. In one are scholars such as Walter Laqueur,[5] who believes that in historical context, terrorism has hardly ever had a lasting effect. Ted Robert Gurr[6] shares Laqueur's conclusions, if not his intellectual disposition, and sees terrorism as an epiphenomenon of short-lived duration that has rarely been particularly effective. In the other camp are writers such as Albert Parry,[7] who sees terrorism as increasingly effective as it ceases to be a remote spectacle and becomes an immediate peril. Others, such as Brian Crozier, emphasize contagion effect,[8] likening terrorism to smallpox and global epidemics. Those who believe terrorism to be effective come from all ideological quarters; there is no apparent correlation between those who see terrorism as effective and any special political viewpoint.

What if we disaggregated the issue of the consequences of terrorism and examined which goals have been achieved and which have been frustrated by terrorism? I define terrorism as the fusion of three properties in an indefinite mix: (1) a type of unconventional warfare engaged in by a group, usually against civilian targets (2) in which violence or threat of violence is employed to induce fear for the purpose of (3) changing the bases of law and authority affecting attitudes, emotions, and opinions through a culturally unacceptable form. If we accept as a given that the major purpose of terrorism is to change a government or

5. Walter Laqueur, "The Futility of Terrorism" and "Second Thoughts on Terrorism," in *The Political Psychology of Appeasement: Finlandization and Other Unpopular Essays* (New Brunswick and London: Transaction/Holt Saunders, 1980), pp. 101–25.

6. Ted Robert Gurr, "Some Characteristics of Political Terrorism in the 1960s," in *The Politics of Terrorism*, ed. Michael Stohl (New York: Marcel Dekker, 1979), pp. 23–49.

7. Albert Parry, *Terrorism: From Robespierre to Arafat* (New York: Vanguard Press, 1976), pp. 55–56.

8. Brian Crozier, *A Theory of Conflict* (New York: Charles Scribner's Sons, 1974), pp. 129–30.

an established authority, and not simply to increase fear or hysteria, then we can assess how successful terrorists are in achieving their goals. For we can certainly establish if terror has brought about the downfall of governments.

Terrorism has emerged partly in relation to the decline in mass political participation. The concentration of power in the hands of a small clique or an elite serves a double-edged purpose: it permits the leader of a nation to employ terrorism as an overseas tactic, as in Libya, and it makes rulers and ruling groups that are less politically integrated vulnerable, as has been the leadership of Egypt. The potential for disrupting the ordinary processes of governance is greatest where mass participation in the political process is lowest. At the same time, terrorist acts are more disruptive to a dictatorship than to a democracy, precisely for the same reason: a dictatorship lacks a broad, mobilized popular support base. Who can doubt that the assassination of Fidel Castro in Cuba would produce far more far-reaching consequences than the elimination of José López Portillo in Mexico?

Although terrorism is most damaging to totalitarian regimes, such regimes are much less vulnerable to terrorism. Precisely because they consider techniques of surveillance and control so important, dictatorships offer their leaders better military and police protection than do democracies. Dictators like Muammar Qadaffi or Castro or Alfredo Stroessner, are virtually impervious to random assaults, unlike, say, American presidents or Catholic pontiffs. Unless a palace guard revolts or is infiltrated, a Caesar's death is unlikely or uncommon. Yet, when such deaths do occur, they have enormous political impact. There is an evident paradox: dictatorships use terrorist methods but can suffer mortal injury from terrorism; and democracies use terrorist methods much less frequently but can easily be permeated and wounded by terrorism.[9] This remains a core problem for those who would define terrorism as a technique of rotating power (as

9. Irving Louis Horowitz, "Can Democracy Cope with Terrorism?" *Civil Liberties Review* 4 (May/June 1977): 29–37.

in parts of the Third World) or as a style of overthrowing systems (as in parts of Western Europe).

It is important to distinguish social from political costs of terrorism. At the social level terrorism has had a dramatic effect on lifestyle: it has supported a surveillance equipment industry, greatly increased investigation and interference with private individuals, and a preference for low-profile (anonymity) rather than high-profile (ostentatious) lifestyles. There have been social costs: increasing privatization and decreasing public participation by elite groups and a corresponding reduction of civil liberties.

Except for regicide (the assassination of senior leaders) terrorist acts have tended to have little impact on political systems. Terrorism has led to better police protection, increased military armaments, and a general popular revulsion against the terrorist. Sometimes the results are politically counterproductive. The decline in electoral strength of Western European communist parties is largely a result of the terrorist phenomenon. The electoral victories of socialist parties in France and Greece, coupled with a decline in Communist party strength and beliefs in both countries, tend to support this.

Terrorism has been successful under the following conditions. First, terrorism has succeeded when tied to nationalism, as in Northern Ireland or the Basque country of Spain. Undisputed claim to territory is the single most important element determining the success or failure of terrorist actions or movements. Even a well-organized and well-financed group such as the Palestine Liberation Organization has felt the absence of a staging area. The PLO's displacement from Syria, then Jordan, and its unsteady relationship with Lebanon have tended to limit its successful use of terrorism against the target population, Israel.

Second, terrorism tends to be successful when linked to specific forms of regicide and unsuccessful when randomly directed. The bombing of a bus or the destruction of physical property, if unattached to clear political objectives, can be counterproductive. In this sense, the level of a terrorist organization's sophistication can largely be defined by its targets. In general, the more focused the target, the more advanced the terrorism; the more random the target, the less effective the terrorism.

The most successful terrorism is linked to the foreign policy of installed regimes. In present-day Libya, the regime sponsors terror and legitimates certain overseas operations. Its ratio of success in these operations can be related to the regime's support; an advantage over the low-intensity adversarial relationships that often exist between governments and terrorist organizations.

Terrorism has been least successful under the following social conditions. When the terrorist group is not connected to a class, race, ethnic, or other institutionalized form of human association, its achievements tend to be desultory and purely ideological. In countries such as Italy, which has had a highly refined terrorist network, the self-segregation of the terrorist organization from the general political process has led to its deep isolation, what the terrorists themselves refer to as "infantilization." Terrorism fails when it is connected to random assassinations, destruction of untargeted property, and unspecified dismemberment of either people or property without regard to who they are or what they represent. Random terror, which has been characteristic of urban terrorism, creates a backlash effect. Finally, when a terrorist organization ceases to exist as a legitimate force that can grow in numbers or recruits, the state police apparatus usually can overwhelm the terrorist organization and all but destroy its effectiveness within the political process.

Admittedly, this brief statement of the conditions under which terrorism is effective is subject to empirical scrutinies of all sorts and from all quarters. One might argue that the assassination of Martin Luther King failed of its purpose in that black mobilization was much higher and federal legislation more vigorous after King's martyrdom than before his death. Still, in the most fundamental sense that the sole unifying leader of black political and religious life had been felled, and with him came the end of the sorts of coalitions with other groups that brought the black communities of America into the political mainstream, one must say on balance that his murder in 1968 no less than the assassination of Robert Kennedy a month later was highly successful. Both deaths killed off any prospect of a center-left administration in the United States in the period 1968–76.

It might also be argued that Libya's international influence derives less from its use of state terrorism than from an accidental advantage of oil riches coupled with United States policies that have permitted Qadaffi to pose as an Arab David against a Western Goliath. It can be further argued that Libya's influence waned considerably with the setbacks it suffered in Uganda and later Chad. But on balance, one would have to say that Libya, in its role as key funding agent of terrorists from the IRA to the PLO, and as resting place and watering hole for terrorist leaders and would-be usurpers of that leadership, was a key factor in the rejectionist front that inspired the assassination of Anwar Sadat and has prevented the Camp David process from reaching maturity.

But whether history-writ-large assesses current forms of terrorism as winners or losers, it is clear enough that terrorism as a tactic has had a dramatic effect on the course of many nations previously thought impregnable to such assaults. When a tactic reaches massive proportions, it can be dismissed as something belonging to the backwaters of politics; for all of its distasteful aspects, terrorism has become a mode of doing politics—a tactic raised to a principle, as it were.

The impact of terrorism is measured on a worldwide rather than on local or regional bases. The killing of Sadat in Cairo, Egypt, set off a wide array of worldwide consequences; a similar assassination a century ago would have had only a local impact. Earlier "anarchist" assaults only rarely had an international impact, as when the assassination of Archduke Ferdinand precipitated World War I. Usually such assassinations may have far-ranging impact but do not even cause a break in diplomatic relations. The wider awareness of terrorist activities is partially a result of improved worldwide data-gathering processes and communication rather than any inherent change in the magnitude of terrorism's impact.

Terrorism is perceived as a multinational dilemma and often as an assault on the legitimacy of the world order. The world seems riskier as a result of terrorism, but terrorism has had the unanticipated consequence of facilitating interdependence between nations, who find they can set aside differences in political orientations in order to preserve and protect the world community of nations. Nationalist and separatist impulses have never been more robust, but the search for world law and for mechanisms for communication across boundaries of political or systemic differences is higher than ever on the agenda of nations.

One way to evaluate the consequences of terrorism is to assess its impact on a society. In this regard the lack of impact of the PLO upon Israeli society is most instructive. Shlomo Gazit, former head of Israeli military intelligence, has said:

The success and effectiveness of our [Israeli] security services and measures and the very low standard of the Palestinian terrorist's professional achievements make the overall impact of this activity on Israel rather limited. Just to give you an idea—during the last fifteen months, beginning in April 1978, we had twenty-eight Israelis killed (civilian and military) by that kind of PLA [Palestine Liberation Activity]. This should be compared to about seven hundred persons killed in road accidents during the same period.[10]

Gazit is discussing the premier terrorist organization in the world, one with a maximum of manpower, weaponry, and funding. Thus, without in any way diminishing the considerable global influence of the PLO, its capacity to inflict direct injury upon Israel or even to threaten the survival of the state remains minimal. Its strength derives from its ability to rein-

10. Shlomo Gazit, "The Myth and Reality of the PLO," in *International Terrorism: Challenge and Response*, ed. Benjamin Netanayhu (New Brunswick: Transaction Books, 1981), pp. 345–46.

force and undergird organized opposition to Israel in other nations and world bodies, not to inflict a mortal blow on its opponent.

In evaluating the PLO claim that it is a guerrilla movement rather than a terrorist cluster of disparate organizations, it is worth remembering that a particular territory (the West Bank and Gaza Strip) has been the sole factor enabling Palestinians to claim self-determination within an intra-Arab context and that this geographical focus has been the foundation that made support for the PLO possible. Indeed, this geographical claim about the boundaries of Palestine provides the common denominator among the some twenty organizations that constitute the PLO. Destroying PLO claims of legitimacy thus becomes Israel's primary target in upsetting the present narrow band of PLO consensus. Whatever the merits or demerits in the PLO approach or the Israeli assault on its geographic claims, it is clear that the thread between land and legitimacy ultimately determines whether this or any other group is defined, in world opinion, as nationalist guerrillas or terrorist outcasts.

Terrorist groups ultimately are engaged in a search for legitimation, an attempt to move up the ladder from terrorism to militarization to insurgency through the destruction of their opponents by any means short of self-immolation. Increased terrorism also increases demands by authorities for the total mobilization of society and the expansion of a national security force. In this sense, terrorism inadvertently tests the health of a state, its ability to survive threat, bluster, and a variety of assaults.

Walter Laqueur's recent assessment of terrorist activities not only demonstrates the limited consequences of terrorism but argues the need for a more ample analytic framework:

A realistic assessment of the terrorist activities over the last ten years would have shown that there has not been much change: in some countries terrorism has been in decline, in others there has been an upsurge. Overall, despite some striking attacks which attracted a great deal of publicity, such as the shooting of the Pope, terrorist groups have been less in the limelight than was the case ten years ago. This is true of Turkey as well as of the Middle East generally, of Latin America, and even of Northern Ireland where the number of victims has declined. Italy is an exception, and there may be one or two others, partly due to the reemergence of extreme right-wing terrorism. All this does not mean that there will not be another rise in such operations in the future, but there is less justification today for treating terrorism as practically the world's most pressing problem.[11]

One may not accept Laqueur's judgments about the difficulties democratic societies have in combating terrorism or the special role of the Soviet "contractor" in respect to clientelist "subcontractors." We need, however, to develop a means to assess the impact of politically sponsored violence. Such a calculus would take into account that terrorism can strengthen rather than weaken organized social and political opposition by the state. Of course every effort to suppress terrorism perforce involves techniques of investigation and intrusion on the privacy of citizens that ultimately weaken the bases of democracy. Israeli commitment to democracy has been weakened by the perceived necessity to respond instantly and massively to PLO terrorism. But high levels of democratic participation still remain. This itself may be an achievement, given the duration and severity of terrorist threats to Israeli survival and sovereignty.

It has been argued that diminished commitment to democracy is a major goal of terrorist organizations; even those with little potential for success are content to destroy democratic institutions and do not really expect that the society or state being opposed will easily crumble. The formulation presumes that terrorists seek to prove a political point rather than gain a military edge. It is true that democratic societies have been forced to curb some marginal rights, but totalitarian societies have not come about as a result of terrorist assaults. To be sure, totalitarian societies preserve power by eliminating opposition political parties, destroying voluntary associations that do not

11. Walter Laqueur, "Reagan and the Russians," *Commentary* 73 (January 1982): 19–26.

serve the state's interests, and preventing spontaneous, individual expressions of difference. Totalitarian societies are unlikely to be toppled by terrorism, which thrives best in the fertile soil of democratic systems. But it does not follow that terrorism necessarily represents a form of class or racial rebellion against oppressive conditions. Terrorism does weaken democracies, but it does not necessarily lessen exploitation or repression. And contrariwise, the absence of terrorism by no means signifies a tranquil or consensually grounded society.

International legislation on issues ranging from controlling air hijackings to strengthening INTERPOL has resulted from a perceived threat to world order. Far from eating away at the vitals of the world political economies, terrorism has reinforced a powerful backlash by legitimate societies. The negative side is that political change has become identified with the illicit methods of achieving it. Terrorism operating in the name of radicalism often generates conservative consequences. But the multinationalization of terrorism is linked more by efforts to sabotage existing regimes than by any common core ideology.[12] If one looks at results, the differences among members of the network become obvious.

That does not mean that it makes sense to try to distinguish between "left" terrorism and "right" terrorism.[13] Terrorism is a unitary phenomenon in practice and in theory. Groups such as Baader Meinhof can and do fuse a variety of jumbled symbols from national liberation to anti-Semitism and work with political systems and regimes extending from the Soviet Union to Libya. To speak of "radicalism" as a revival of participatory democracy and "terrorism" as a simple resort to violence[14] is to miss the essential multinational mix. Believing that neo-Nazi

12. Claire Sterling, *The Terror Network: The Secret War of International Terrorism* (New York: Reader's Digest Press/Holt, Rinehart, and Winston, 1981); and Samuel T. Francis, *The Soviet Strategy of Terror* (Washington, D.C.: Heritage Foundation, 1981).

13. Irving Louis Horowitz, "Left-Wing Fascism: An Infantile Disorder," *Transaction/Society* 18 (May/June 1981): 19–24.

14. Sheldon Wolin, "Separating Terrorism from Radicalism," *New York Times*, November 3, 1981; and Victor Navasky, "Security and Terrorism," *The Nation*, February 14, 1981, p. 168.

activity is directed from Moscow may comfort those who would like to place terrorism in one corner of the political spectrum, but it misses the essential character of terrorism as such, its antistatist characteristics, its categorical eschewal of democratic and legal norms for changing regimes and policies. Abstractions such as "the international Zionist conspiracy" provide a blanket ideology for terrorists on the left and the right, from Europe to Africa, an ideology that permits a wide latitude of meanings and hence participants.

Political systems, like people, compete with each other, and they sometimes exceed the boundaries of peaceful competition. Because terrorism is a twentieth-century plague infecting all social systems, the resulting development of mechanisms to ensure the political survival of systems as such can create new forms of international association. For example, except for the PLO, relationships between Israeli and Lebanese border communities could scarcely have developed. The routinization of terrorism as a multinational problem cannot be denied, but political organisms have shown an increased capacity to unite and create a new basis for legitimacy. Routinized terror makes political risks higher, but it also increases the rewards of political legitimacy.

Terrorism does weaken democracy, the structural victim of terrorism. The cycle may begin with a terrorist kidnapping or killing, followed by the enactment, enforcement, or strengthening of antiterrorist laws and a corresponding suspension of constitutional safeguards. The third stage is the acceleration of terrorist activities in the name of overturning despotic rule. Legislation that restricts human freedoms sometimes precedes rather than follows terrorist assaults, but the same cycle ensues—only with a different causal starting point. Whatever the personal victims of terrorist assaults, the collective victims are the citizenry and constitutional safeguards.

As a tactic terrorism has failed to reach its primary objective, changing the foundations of state power, and for that reason it has earned the scorn of revolutionaries no less than the wrath of conservatives. It has had mixed success in achieving its sec-

ondary objectives: being taken seriously by established authority, obtaining high media coverage, and insinuating itself as a
factor in negotiations concerning critical geopolitical areas. In
its tertiary goals terrorism has been especially effective: it has
reduced the operational range of democratic societies, has com-
pelled democratic societies to curb essential freedoms in the
name of survival, and in so doing, has provided support to its
prophecy that democracy is vulnerable and democratic societies are hypocritical with respect to their claims of political
superiority.

One might well argue for a system some midway point between democracy and dictatorship that could measure and
monitor terrorist acts. Policy proposals are not lacking: stronger
weapons controls, computerized surveillance systems, juridical limits on civil compliance with illegal demands, censorship
of mass media to prevent undue publicity for terrorist activities, and so on. Such midway systems would in fact erode the
democratic process. Policy-oriented safety devices against terror are too easily extended to tools for institutional constraints
upon the body politic. Informal constraints become normative
limits to democratic decision-making.

Those who would support general policies countering terror
with paramilitary structures must be willing to bear the consequences of a world without democracy; just as those who
would countenance a purely Hobbesian world of anarchic competition of lawless individuals must bear the burdens of a world
lacking in organization or coherence. Those who would exag-
gerate tactics, either as laissez-faire approaches toward terror or
as heavy-handed regimentation to prevent terror, must equally
come to terms with the imperfections of democracy and the
infections of dictatorship.

Seen in this way the consequences of terrorism have little to
do with the rise and fall of societies and a great deal to do with
the limits each society imposes on the civil liberties of its citizenry in order to secure its survival. Nondemocratic societies
are more brittle and more vulnerable to destruction than democratic societies. But the attempt to meet the challenge of terror-

ism by a heightened defense posture and increased security measures converts democratic societies into garrison states or into a new feudalism in which security firms usurp public police power, often widening rather than limiting the scope of lawless operations.[15] This vicious dialectic can be broken down in two ways: by the absolute crushing of opposition, as in totalitarian systems, or by accepting the risks of terror as a permanent feature of developed, mobile, and liberal societies, as necessary evils along with prostitution, gambling, drugs, and other forms of deviance. Policy options take on meaning only in the context of what elements of its political soul a society is willing to risk. It is important to understand the successes and failures of terrorism so that we can assess policy options—and risks—in a real world context. We may decide that terrorism is but one of the many continuing curses that must be borne if the democratic balance wheel itself is to endure.

Even if we can reach a consensus about the sources of terrorism, that it reflects elite rather than mass discontent, personal dislocations rather than deep social cleavages, we cannot move directly to a policy designed to eliminate terrorism without a much clearer notion of the likely social consequences. For example, how much militarism is the American public likely to accept in efforts to curb domestic terrorism?[16] Just as benign tumors sometimes look like critical cancers, varieties of terrorism may also "look alike" but function differentially in a variety of social contexts. One must pay careful attention to such distinctions, not just to satisfy bad academic habits of nitpicking but to justify a continuing quest for democracy in a political universe of expanding social uncertainty.

15. James A. Nathan, "The New Feudalism," *Foreign Policy* 42 (Spring 1981): 156–66.
16. William R. Farrell, "Military Involvement in Domestic Terror Incidents," *Naval War College Review* (July/August 1981) 34: 53–66.

Anthony C. E. Quainton

3

Terrorism
and Political Violence:
A Permanent Challenge
to Governments

The sesquicentennial of a great university is an appropriate occasion to reflect on the salient problems that beset our world: a
time both to look back with a due sense of history and to look
forward to the challenges which institutions and individuals
face as they approach the twenty-first century. High on the list
of such challenges is the threat which political violence and
terrorism represents to the creation of a stable, peaceful, and
democratic world order.

Notwithstanding the fact that official statistics on terrorism
go back only to the late 1960s, terrorism as a phenomenon did
not begin with the slaying of the first (of five) American ambassadors in 1968. To be sure, those assassinations, together with
the hijackings of the early 1970s and the hostage incidents at
the 1972 Munich Olympic Games, at the 1975 OPEC meeting,
and at the American Embassy in Teheran in 1979 made the
1970s into "Terror Decade I," as Claire Sterling put it in her

recent bestseller, *The Terror Network*.[1] In that decade, indeed, terrorism became part of America's popular political vocabulary. It was not the first such decade, but it was a unique period in which the United States became the principal target of terrorist violence. Thirty-seven percent of the more than seven thousand recorded international terrorist incidents worldwide involved Americans or American property. No other country had to face such a variety or intensity of terrorist attack.

Because we were the principal terrorist target and the principal victims of political violence, the 1970s was also a period in which the U.S. government organized itself to combat this phenomenon. The creation in the autumn of 1972 of an Interagency Working Group on Terrorism, reporting directly to a Cabinet Committee on Terrorism, was evidence of that new concern. That working group, which originally encompassed only a dozen agencies, grew by the end of the Carter administration to an organization with more than thirty members. Virtually all agencies of government from the Post Office to the CIA were directly involved in the effort to mobilize the U.S. government's resources in the battle against terrorist violence. Even nonfederal agencies and groups such as the National League of Cities, the National Governors Association, and the Washington metropolitan police became active members and thereby brought into the planning effort the unique perspective of state and local governments.

The Carter administration modified these structures and abolished the cabinet committee. In its place it created an executive committee of the working group reporting directly to the National Security Council. This executive committee, composed of the State, Defense, Justice, Treasury, and Energy departments as well as representatives of the FBI, CIA, FAA, the Joint Chiefs of Staff, and the National Security Council staff, formed a small group of key agencies each with significant responsibilities in the counterterrorism area.

The Reagan administration further streamlined the system

1. New York: Reader's Digest Press/Holt, Rinehart, and Winston, 1981.

by concentrating the interagency effort in an interdepartmental Group on Terrorism. This group, like its predecessors, remained under State Department chairmanship but now reports to the president through the secretary of state rather than through the National Security Council system. All of those structures, as modified by subsequent administrations, have been designed to ensure effective coordination of policies and plans as well as a rapid and effective government response to the challenge of terror violence.

However new and threatening political violence appeared in 1972, it had its roots deep in history.[2] In its terrorist incarnation it goes back at least to the formation in 1878 in Russia of Narodnaya Volya (the People's Will). That group, bent on the disruption and ultimate overthrow of the tsarist system, chose as its targets the very symbols of Russian authority, the tsar, his family, and high officials of his government. Like all subsequent terrorist groups, the People's Will used violence or the threat of violence against symbolic targets to publicize its cause and to influence political behavior. Over the ensuing century, bombings, assassinations, and kidnappings became a routine part of the political order. Presidents, prime ministers, and even the pope were targeted. The targets varied as did the tactics and the weapons, but the basic fact remained that systematic violence was used as an instrument of social and political change. Modern terrorism, involving the unscrupulous use of innocent victims for political extortion, is only a refinement on age-old tactics of intimidation, intrigue, and assassination.

Although contemporary terrorism is often thought of as a phenomenon primarily involving individuals and small groups, throughout history governments have also used force, intimidation, and violence for their political purposes to oppress and dominate their subjects, to defeat their enemies, or to enhance their national power. In those forms political violence achieved a certain legitimacy. But only when technology advanced to a

2. A historical perspective is found in Walter Laqueur, *Terrorism* (Boston: Little, Brown, 1977).

point where the instruments of violence threatened civilization itself did the international community begin to make a serious effort to limit its impact. The development of chemical and biological weapons and the possibility of nuclear holocaust have raised even more complex issues of moral legitimacy with respect to the use of force.

The rise of terrorism over the last century has sharpened our focus on the problem of identifying those forms of violence which are illegitimate even when used on behalf of morally admirable causes. Until the mid-nineteenth century national self-interest dominated international relations. Political scientists and international lawyers were concerned with the behavior of states. In the twentieth century, however, they have had to take into account the activities of a bewildering array of sub-state actors, many of whom are formed into what we now call terrorist groups. Often supported and encouraged by nation-states, these groups have taken on an independent existence and thereby are able to pose new challenges to the international community in general and to our government in particular.

Terrorist groups seek to change the political system by force; yet they lack the status that attaches to nation-states. Although the international community has generally accepted the legitimacy of national liberation struggles against colonial regimes, it has not, nor should it, accept the targeting of the nation-state itself. Those ethnic terrorists who seek to take the Basques out of Spain, the Croatians out of Yugoslavia, or the Moluccans out of Indonesia enjoy little international support. The disruption of the national unity of the countries concerned, like the violent overthrow of democratic systems by radical groups such as the Red Brigades, is intrinsically illegitimate. So it should remain.

If terrorist strategies are controversial, even more so are their tactics. When terrorists bomb, kill, or kidnap on behalf of revolution or in support of national liberation, many argue that the ends justify the means. They assert that the causes are morally and legally defensible and that the situations giving rise to these liberation struggles are so unjust and oppressive as to justify any tactic. This argument is one with which democratic societies have difficulty in dealing. Yet if we wish to create a less violent world order some way must be found to delegitimize terrorist violence and to separate means from ends. If we cannot, violence will remain a permanent factor in national and international life.

The challenge for the statesman and the politician is how to limit that violence and how to build a moral and political consensus to oppose terrorism whenever and wherever it violates fundamental moral values. A generation ago, Benito Mussolini, in an effort to justify the actions of his fascist goon squads, wrote: "There is a violence that liberates, and there is a violence that enslaves; there is moral violence and stupid, immoral violence."[3] Throughout the Third World today there are those who proclaim the liberating and cathartic value of violence but who fail to accept the proposition that reliance on it as an instrument of political change can ultimately lead only to political servitude and that a violence which proclaims itself the defender of moral values is more likely than not to lead to immoral exploitation. As the terrorist has spoken for the legitimacy of violence over the last century, governments have increasingly recognized the moral and practical limitations of the use of force. They have become less tolerant of all forms of disruptive violence, but particularly of terrorist violence.

To the extent that violence is a prominent feature of our world and is likely to remain so in the decades ahead, governments must decide how to organize themselves to deal with it. A credible long-term response must have at least five dimensions: law enforcement, social and economic reform, moral suasion, a deterrent policy, and media restraint. No one element offers a complete answer; each reinforces the others. Together they hold out the prospect of reducing both the quantum and the ferocity of political violence.

The most obvious and least controversial response is law en-

3. Speech in Udine, September 20, 1922.

forcement. Within societies most terrorist acts are criminal in character and are so designated in the legal code. Although an assassination, or a bombing, or a kidnapping may take place with a political motive, that does not diminish the fact that the act is a violation of domestic criminal statutes. Although each country has its own standards and rules of law, many basic elements are the same. All governments recognize that law enforcement agencies must have adequate sources of intelligence and vigorous investigative techniques. Rapid response capabilities are needed. The penal and judicial systems must contain the necessary legislative sanctions so that the perpetrators of terrorist acts can be promptly brought to justice.

Intelligence is the first and in some ways the critical element. It is not only a means of forewarning but also a necessary adjunct of response. When forewarned of terrorist plans, police can act to protect the target, to interdict the perpetrators, and to prevent and defeat the attack. The 1981 Libyan threat to the president and other senior leaders was an example of the importance of intelligence to our national security.

But good intelligence will never be available in adequate depth, and no law enforcement agency can rely on it to the exclusion of other methods. One of the reasons for the relatively low level of political violence in the United States is the accurate perception that the FBI and other members of the law enforcement community possess large and effective resources with which to pursue the perpetrators of a terrorist act. They will deploy SWAT and other specialized teams as necessary to ensure that terrorists do not obtain their objectives through hostage-taking or other violent techniques.

The judicial system must be equally resolute. The seriousness of a crime should not be mitigated out of sympathy with a particular cause. This is especially important in extradition cases where the political defense exception is widely used. Terrorists' claims that their violent acts are intrinsically political must be resisted. The criminal nature of terrorism must be kept to the forefront of our legal response.

Unfortunately, at the present time, in many countries terrorists face weak law enforcement capabilities and hesitant and cumbersome judicial proceedings. The practice of terrorism is frequently a low-risk proposition. Often the perpetrators are not caught or are allowed to flee to some external safe haven. Even if caught and brought to justice, they receive light sentences reflecting more the glamour of their trade than the seriousness of their crime. The weakness of society's response is, in fact, an incentive to further violence.

Important though law enforcement may be, no society can rely exclusively on the police to resolve the problem of political violence. The causes of that violence must also be addressed. In our world this means that where possible political, social, or economic grievances must be met head-on. In some contexts this will be difficult. The international system obviously cannot tolerate the dismemberment or destruction of existing nation-states to suit the convenience of Basque, or Irish, or Palestinian, or Croatian terrorists. The social and economic system cannot be reordered merely to meet the revolutionary ideology of the Red Army Faction, the Red Brigades, or the Japanese Red Army. That is not to say, however, that over the next two decades an earnest effort need not be made to find imaginative solutions to aspirations for autonomy, independence, or unity, nor that social and economic reforms need not take place even in democratic societies. These tasks should be high on the agenda of diplomats and politicians. Certainly in the Middle East, in southern Africa, and in Central America, the root causes of terrorism are already major priorities of our foreign policy.

The sources of violence in our world will not only be political. Population pressures, competition for scarce resources, and income disequilibria are certain to provide the breeding ground for future violence and terrorism. The developed world's resources, both governmentally and privately channeled and contributed, should be creatively deployed. For only in conditions of relative prosperity and growth can the world hope to see the curve of violence turn downward. But we cannot have any illusions about the time frame involved. None of the principal social and economic problems of the Third World and few of these same issues in the developed world can be solved rapidly. Patience, perseverance, and imagination will be the hallmarks of success. And in the short run as expectations rise we may have to face heightened political instability and violence.

In addition to short-term police action and long-term political, economic, and social reforms the moral dimension of violence should also be addressed. The prevalence of violence in the world can, from a religious perspective, be seen as a reflection of original sin. But whether one accepts that view or not, there is no doubt of the deep human predisposition to violence. The more important question is how that predisposition can be channeled and controlled.

One answer is to focus on the varieties of violence that all condemn. In the laws of war the world has already made considerable progress in outlawing torture, genocide, and the use of chemical and biological agents. International conventions dealing with these techniques enjoy broad, almost universal support, reflecting a deep international consensus that their use is unjustifiable in civilized societies. The Geneva Conventions of 1949 were designed to protect civilians in time of war. A comparable effort has been made to protect civilians from terrorist attacks, because the cynical exploitation of civilian targets is a distinctive feature of modern-day terrorism.

In the absence of any internationally accepted definition of terrorism, the world community has concentrated on outlawing the specific acts that have occurred most frequently and have been used most destructively: assassination, hijacking, and hostage-taking.[4] As early as 1937 in the aftermath of the assassination of King Alexander of Yugoslavia, the League of Nations adopted a convention for the prevention or punishment of terrorism. This convention focused on assassinations and attacks on heads of state as well as on acts "calculated to endanger the lives of the members of the public." In the 1930s

4. The texts of these documents can be found in Yonah Alexander, Marjorie Ann Browne, and Allan S. Nanes, eds., *Control of Terrorism: International Documents* (New York: Crane, Russak, 1979).

nations were so preoccupied with the drift toward war in Europe that that convention never came into effect and indeed was ratified by only one state—India.

Nonetheless, the concept of codifying the international community's abhorrence of certain kinds of violence did not wither and indeed took on new life in the 1960s and 1970s. Under the impact of hijackings and other violent and unlawful acts against civil aviation, conventions were adopted in Tokyo in 1963, The Hague in 1970, and Montreal in 1971. All provide for the prosecution or extradition of the perpetrators of the proscribed offenses. All require that the acts be dealt with as serious common crimes for which governments have an obligation to ensure punishment. None, however, contains any enforcement mechanisms despite repeated efforts by the United States (most recently at a conference in Rome in 1973) to obtain agreement on the automatic imposition of aviation sanctions (the suspension of air services) against states that fail to observe their obligations under the Hague and Montreal conventions.

A second consensus has emerged about crimes against diplomats or other internationally protected persons. Historically, diplomats have enjoyed special status under international law. This status, however, has steadily eroded to the point where diplomats and the premises in which they work are more often attacked than any other category of target. In the period 1968–81 there have been 2,688 such attacks, or a third of all recorded international terrorist events. Not only have twenty ambassadors and more than one hundred other diplomats been killed, but the embassies of thirty-eight countries have been seized. Dozens more have been subject to bombing or gunfire. In 1980 alone there were more than four hundred attacks against diplomats in sixty countries. In response to this trend, first the Organization of American States in 1971 and then the United Nations in 1973 adopted conventions outlawing attacks on internationally protected persons including diplomatic agents. These conventions have provided only part of the answer. Reinforced security and special protective measures have become the norm for diplomats serving abroad. Even with these measures we must expect diplomacy to remain a major symbolic target.

Finally, at the end of the decade, as concern with hostage-taking grew, an ad hoc committee appointed by the United Nations General Assembly drafted a convention on hostage-taking. This convention, adopted without opposition in December 1979, extended to yet another category of terrorist acts the requirement that perpetrators be brought to justice. This convention, the earlier New York Convention of 1973, and the almost universal international condemnation of Iran's seizure of the American Embassy in Teheran are evidence of a growing willingness by governments to oppose and act against diplomatic hostage situations.

Despite these efforts, hostage-taking remains a major weapon of terrorist groups. We have not yet achieved a reduction in hostage incidents comparable to the diminution of attacks against civil aviation that took place after the adoption of the Hague and Montreal conventions. Nonetheless, the international community is continuing its efforts to convince terrorist groups and their patrons that these tactics are inadmissible and counterproductive and will meet a concerted international response.

But even assuming effective law enforcement, a willingness to come to grips with the underlying social and political causes, and efforts to widen the scope of international law, violence will continue. The ready availability of the tools of the trade, be they pistols, submachine guns, or rocket launchers, combined with the continued success of terrorists to obtain the release of prisoners, the payment of ransom, and the publication of manifestos ensure that the international community will face acts of terrorism in the future.

The measures discussed above should be part of a longer-term strategy designed to raise the costs and lower the benefits terrorists obtain from their acts. If the benefits are truly to be reduced, however, two other steps will have to be taken: a deterrent policy will have to be adopted and the media will have to exercise restraint. As long as terrorist groups can count on substantive concessions, a press willing to sensationalize terrorist acts, and ultimate safe passage to a country of refuge, terrorist tactics will be an attractive option.

Governments will first have to decide and publicly proclaim that they will not meet terrorists' substantive demands, particularly in incidents of duration involving the taking of hostages. In fact, many governments, while pugnacious in their rhetoric, have been pusillanimous in their actions—paying ransoms, freeing prisoners, and granting publicity. The United States government is one of very few never to have paid a political ransom.

The private sector supports a strong government response but has not in general stood firm in the face of threats to its own employees. Kidnap insurance is common, and corporations frequently ransom their kidnapped employees, buy space for terrorist propaganda, and oppose the use of force against their premises or their aircraft. The short-term goal of saving lives invariably transcends concerns about the longer-term consequences for democratic societies of concessional behavior.[5]

But even if governments, corporations, and citizens were in agreement in opposing concessions, there would remain a problem of media coverage. Terrorism is a source of tremendous public interest, which will inevitably be exploited by the press and the electronic media. The issue that confronts policymakers is how and to what extent that media interest can be focused on the threat terrorism represents for free societies.

No subject is more sensitive in a free society than control or manipulation of the press. Yet the issue must be faced on at least two levels: the media's high tolerance for violence in general and its glamorization and sensationalization of specific violent acts. Although it is not possible to prove a direct relationship between the electronic media's exploitation of vio-

5. The private sector's view of this issue is expressed in several articles in Yonah Alexander and Robert A. Kilmarx, eds., *Political Terrorism and Business* (New York: Praeger, 1979); see particularly Julian Radcliffe, "The Insurance Companies' Response to Terrorism," pp. 151–60.

lence and the overall incidence of violence in society, there is sufficient evidence to suggest that the repeated depiction of violent behavior desensitizes individuals and creates a climate within which violence is seen as normal rather than aberrational social behavior.

More specifically, in terrorist incidents the tendency to focus on the individual terrorist with the grudging admiration we reserve for skilled practitioners of a sport, encourages the terrorist to believe he can obtain not only a personal apotheosis but also the public recognition and vital publicity his cause requires to survive and grow. If we are serious about reducing the incidence of political violence in democratic societies, sooner or later something will have to be done to reduce the glamour of violence and to persuade the media to accept either self-regulation or some more formal government control as an integral part of a broad counterterrorist strategy.

Even to suggest some limited restrictions on press freedom, however, raises fundamental questions of constitutional rights. It also points to the difficulty democratic governments face in defining their response to terrorism and in setting clear priorities for dealing with it. The repression of violence, whether criminal or political, national or international, has been a relatively low priority for most governments. Certainly the history of violence in our own society over the last two generations makes clear that we have pursued other priorities. With a naive utopianism, many have asserted that prosperity and economic growth would lead to a world without war and by extension to one without terrorism as well. We have not developed a comprehensive strategy that looks on the issue of violence as a long-term and fundamental challenge to democratic values. This we must do. We must also see violence as something that can be grappled with comprehensively and concretely using moral suasion, humane yet effective law enforcement, and media restraint.

Those who support, train, or give comfort to the perpetrators of violence must also be made to feel the full force of international opposition and opprobrium. More than moral posturing is needed; nations must be prepared to isolate and ostracize the patrons of violence. The Libyas, the Cubas, and the South Yemens of this world must be put on notice by all nations that support democratic values that encouragement and support of terrorism can no longer be countenanced. Wherever possible, bilateral and multilateral sanctions should be imposed on those states that actively use terror violence to destabilize the international political system.

Against this background, what has been the U.S. government's response? For a decade the priority succeeding administrations have attached to combating terrorism has risen steadily. The elements of the response have been remarkably constant. We have sought to develop the most competent array of police and intelligence capabilities consistent with our Constitution. We have supported and ratified all international conventions in this field and have taken the lead in encouraging others to do the same. We have articulated and lived up to a clear and unequivocal no-concessions policy. We have greatly enhanced the security systems that protect our president, our diplomats, and other sensitive symbolic targets. We have developed military response capabilities second to none. We have taken economic and political measures against the terrorist patron states.

The perpetrators of violence should be in no doubt that the United States is engaged in a serious worldwide effort to combat the use of terrorist violence. We engage in this effort because we are convinced that only resolute and sustained policies will save the democratic and pluralistic institutions which we are dedicated to defend and on which our national security depends. Although we know that complete success is uncertain, given the permanence of violence, a commitment to combat terrorism and other forms of political violence is essential to a more stable, peaceful, and democratic world order.

Yehezkel Dror

4

Terrorism as a Challenge to the Democratic Capacity to Govern[1]

Terms of Reference

The subject of terrorism combines harsh moral choices, scientific significance, public fascination, political repercussions, and policy grimness. From the perspective of ethics, the "tragic choices"[2] forced upon societies and rulers by terrorism are very harsh; high costs are associated with all alternatives. From a scientific perspective, terrorism is an unusual, though not extraordinary, phenomenon with some features of an extreme case.[3] The study of terrorism may permit insights into broader

1. I am grateful to the Russell Sage Foundation, New York, and the Institute for Advanced Study, Berlin, for providing stimulating environments in which this paper could take shape; and to Wesleyan University for providing the impetus and opportunity for its preparation. Special thanks are due to the organizer of the conference, Martha Crenshaw, and to many of the participants, whose comments contributed much to this paper.

2. This concept is taken from Guido Calabresi and Phillip Bobbitt, *Tragic Choice* (New York: Norton, 1979), who apply it in a different context. Their formulations provide a good key for considering some of the awful moral choices imposed by terrorism.

3. Terrorism has a long history, but its contemporary importance is closely tied to specific features of modernity, such as weapons and transportation tech-

psychological, political, societal, and other types of behavior—going beyond knowledge that can be acquired through investigating more "normal" reality. Public attention is mesmerized by the dramatics of terrorism, mixed with enough anxiety to provide a tingle of personal excitement and with enough distance to reassure that it will not happen here and now. Politically, terrorism poses one more challenge to governments and rulers already overloaded quantitatively and qualitatively; it constitutes both a danger of failure with immediate and long-term consequences and an opportunity to reassert the requisites of a viable democratic capacity to govern. Terrorism demonstrates some main features of modern policy predicaments, posing an additional challenge to policy-making capacities and serving as an indicator of the present quality of policy-making.[4] Little wonder that the literature on terrorism is booming with a mixture of serious studies and fictional treatments, sometimes with hard-to-discern borders between them.[5]

Still, our ignorance far surpasses our knowledge. What are the aggregate and specific causes of the various forms of terrorism? What are its effects, especially its second-order consequences and diffuse impacts? What factors determine the probability of terrorists employing "unconventional" means in one way or another? These are just a few random samples from the large sets of ignorance on terrorism. In part, this ignorance results from the "spread" of the term "terrorism," which

---

nologies, human rights, and liberal values. Terrorism can serve as an important case study of the permanence and elasticity in social phenomena. Some first steps in this direction are taken by Walter Laqueur in *Terrorism: A Study of National and International Political Violence* (Boston: Little, Brown, 1977), but no comprehensive historical-contextual study of terrorism is as yet available. Much writing on terrorism is shallow, cashing in on its drama.

4. This perspective is further developed in Yehezkel Dror, *Public Policy-making Reexamined: A Second Look* (New Brunswick: Transaction Books, 1983).

5. See Augustus R. Norton and Martin H. Greenberg, *International Terrorism: An Annotated Bibliography and Research Guide* (Boulder, Colo.: Westview, 1980). Yonah Alexander, ed., *Terrorism: An International Journal* (New York: Crane Russak), also provides a good sample of writings, as well as comprehensive literature coverage. I avoid extensive references to the literature on terrorism, preferring instead to guide the interested reader to writings on governance and policy analysis.

means many different things to many different people;[6] in part from the unavailability of necessary data, shrouded in secrecy. But, I think, this ignorance principally stems from the state of the social sciences, which lack the frames of appreciation, cognitive maps, concept packages, and methodology to comprehend complex phenomena that cannot be understood through decomposition into easier-to-analyze subelements. Our generation, like earlier generations, is overwhelmed by events we cannot adequately comprehend with contemporary modes of thinking and tacit models.[7] Social sciences may be accused of hiding behind sorcery[8] instead of becoming more sophisticated.

Ambitions for understanding terrorism must, in consequence, be restrained. Getting lost in large data banks is not much better than escaping into ideological explanations. Nor do we really understand other complex phenomena such as drug addiction, religious movements, or sharp changes in political climates. Even economic behavior, which we thought had given up its secrets to our clever models, is again escaping into the realm of the puzzling. Admitting that much about terrorism is unknown and unknowable with present intellectual capacities and equipment is, therefore, nothing very special. Problems in considering and analyzing clinically so "red hot" a subject as terrorism add another barrier to understanding and effective treatment. This is no counsel of despair, but rather a caveat to limit aspirations, to be skeptical about "common sense" as well as "scientific" findings, and to adopt a learning posture in developing counterterrorism policies.

I am concerned here with terrorism as a challenge to the

6. Missing from the literature are studies of the uses and misuses of the term "terrorism" as well as of its changing meanings. Richard Koebner and Helmut Dan Schmidt, *Imperialism: The Story and Significance of a Political Word, 1840–1960* (Cambridge: Cambridge University Press, 1964), serves as an example of what should be attempted with respect to the verbal symbol "terrorism."

7. Compare this to efforts by Italian Renaissance thinkers to understand historic transformations. See J. G. A. Pocock, *The Machiavellian Movement: Florentine Political Thought and the Atlantic Republican Tradition* (Princeton: Princeton University Press, 1975).

8. Stanislav Andreski, *Social Sciences as Sorcery* (New York: St. Martin's Press, 1972). Although overstated in parts, his comments apply with particular force to many writings on terrorism.

democratic capacity to govern and with developing broad-level counterterrorism "grand-policies" for governments to follow. Several policy options will be illustrated as a conclusion. My purpose is to preview the policy analysis of terrorism by looking at terrorism within the context of democratic capacities to govern. I also wish to explore the connections between policy analysis methodologies and the development of strategies against terrorism.[9]

Because of the heterogeneous contents of the term "terrorism" as it is used in different worlds of discourse, it is impossible to arrive at any single definition. "Terrorism" here refers to the use of selective intense violence by small groups to undermine democratic government, to bring about changes (usually ill-defined) in regime and society, and to force governments to adopt dictated decisions of a political and/or economic nature. By limiting myself to terrorism against democratic regimes, I avoid most of the mix-ups, divergences, and value-dependent disagreements on "terrorists" versus "freedom fighters."[10] I also choose to forego the specifics of country responses to terrorism and to focus on generalizations about constant and shared features. Since such analysis necessarily neglects some stubborn realities, its application to specific countries requires significant adjustments. Abstract theories are an essential counterpart to the proliferation of microstudies, but there are limits to their value. Because differences between "terrorism" in diverse cultures and political systems are so large as to make all-inclusive treatments doubtful, this essay is limited to terrorism in democracies.

9. The predicaments of terrorism can serve as a good test case of policy analysis. Preliminary evaluation indicates some weaknesses of most policy analysis, especially in handling the more qualitative and diffuse, but crucial, aspects of terrorism and options for counterterrorism.

10. It is hard to avoid the conclusion that uses and misuses of the concept of terrorism when applied to nondemocratic countries make it useless, if not counterproductive, to understanding and treatment. The problem goes far beyond "concept stretching" (Giovanni Sartori, "European Political Parties: The Case of Polarized Pluralism," in Robert Dahl and Dean Neubauer, eds., *Modern Political Analysis* [Englewood Cliffs, N.J.: Prentice-Hall, 1968], pp. 114–49). It might be better to substitute the concept of "atrocity."

Forms and Causes of Terrorism in Democracies

Three principal and two secondary forms of terrorism in democracies can be distinguished: (1) Native terrorism, by locals and for local objectives. Ethnic autonomy, changes in external and domestic policies, and revolutionary weakening of the state illustrate the main nominal goals of native terrorism in democratic countries. (2) Imported terrorism, by and on behalf of aliens. Changes in external policies, pressures on third parties to meet demands by the terrorist groups, and "revenge" for insults and injuries illustrate the goals of imported terrorism. (3) Transient terrorism, by aliens and against aliens, on the territory of the democracy, but not directed against it. A large variety of conflicts, ideologies, and aspirations may lie behind it. (4) Terrorism against groups or entities within a democracy but not directed against the state or government. (5) Extraterritorial terrorism, against external representatives, persons, properties, and symbols of the democracy. Usually such terrorism is perpetrated by aliens, with or without various degrees of support and backing by the local government, who make monetary, foreign policy, economic, and symbolic demands. Extraterritorial terrorism by citizens of the target democracy is also possible.

This brief typology demonstrates the great difficulty of eliminating or even significantly reducing terrorism through eradicating its causes.[11] Not only are the motives of terrorism, as distinct from nominal causes, unknown and closely interwoven with basic societal processes, but the multiplicity of forms and causes of terrorism makes root treatment nearly impossible. This does not mean that in some specific cases, where there is strong reason to think that a correlation and also a causal relation exists between changeable variables and terrorism, elimination or reduction of the causes of that form of ter-

---

11. This conclusion can be drawn from any serious study of the causes of terrorism. See Martha Crenshaw, "The Causes of Terrorism," *Comparative Politics* 13 (July 1981): 379–99.

rorism may not be a preferable counter terrorism policy. But, this is a rare situation.

Proposition No. 1. Terrorism in democracies cannot generally be handled through elimination of its causes.

This proposition rejects the simple sloganism of "let us get rid of the causes of terrorism and it will wither away on its own." It exposes the basic intellectual difficulty of coping with a problem whose basic causes are largely beyond understanding and beyond treatment. This problem reflects a basic predicament of policy-making and demonstrates a fundamental and paradigmatic challenge to the capacity to govern: in-depth causes are beyond useful knowledge. Pragmatic symptom-treatment is usually useless and frequently counterproductive. It is politically difficult to accept and adopt demanding policies that are doubtful in their consequences.

We should look at terrorism as a test case of the democratic capacity to govern. Many present and expected challenges to democracies are harsher and more difficult than the relatively minor issue of terrorism. The inability to handle terrorism, therefore, indicates serious weakness in the overall democratic capacity to govern. Successful policies toward terrorism can constitute a learning process for building up general democratic governing abilities.

Proposition No. 2. The handling of terrorism can serve as a test case of the democratic capacity to govern.[12]

Impacts of Terrorism on Democracies

In many respects, the handling of terrorism in democracies is an impressive success story.[13] Few Western democracies have stumbled or faltered because of terrorism, even in the face of assassinations of key officials. No central policy appears to

12. My ongoing study *On the Incapacity to Govern* deals at greater length with terrorism as a test case of the capacity to govern.
13. No comprehensive comparative study has been published, but see Juliet Lodge, ed., *Terrorism: A Challenge to the State* (New York: St. Martin's Press, 1981); and Ernest Evans, *Calling a Truce to Terror: The American Response to International Terrorism* (Westport, Conn.: Greenwood Press, 1979).

have been abandoned to accommodate terrorist demands. The financial costs and the physical inconveniences of protecting targets and conducting surveillance seem bearable after one gets used to them. In actuarian calculus, the risk of being harmed by terrorists is lower than of being hit in a car accident, even in the most intensely affected democracies. The human costs of terrorism, however tragic, are small. Given the failures of governments in many other policy domains, their success in handling terrorism deserves special attention. The relative simplicity of the operational containment of damage; expertise of governments, of police, of intelligence, and of the military; and the attention paid to the dramatic issue of terrorism may explain this apparent success.

Proposition No. 3. Democracies have been successful in containing terrorism and in limiting its direct damage.

Broad and insidious effects of terrorism on democracies may result from synergistic interaction between terrorism and other forms of strain. Combined stresses may even endanger the survival of democracies—as seen in the Weimar Republic, Uruguay, and Turkey.[14] In such cases terrorism cannot be isolated from the other variables with which it interacts, but it seems that terrorism may cause much deeper and persistent damage than revealed by manifest symptoms. Though we must guess at the specific contribution of terrorism to the deterioration of democracy, inhibiting terrorism may break vicious circles of decline before they get out of control.

Proposition No. 4. Terrorism can cause serious harm to democracies, especially in combination with other factors that erode and strain democracy. In weak democracies, terrorism can be pivotal in undermining the regime by aggravating strains and weakening fault lines.

14. See Juan L. Linz and Alfred Stepan, eds., *The Breakdown of Democratic Regimes* (Baltimore: Johns Hopkins University Press, 1978); and Edy Kaufman, *Uruguay in Transition: From Civilian to Military Rule* (New Brunswick: Transaction Books, 1979). Additional comparative studies on the breaking points of democracies, including the impact of terrorism, are urgently needed. This paper deals with democracies not because nondemocracies are better off or are distinguished by higher governmental capabilities but because this is my subject.

This proposition is not susceptible to clear proof or falsification, at least with presently available data and research methods. Detailed country case studies may provide some specific findings,[15] though time spans are still too short for convincing evidence to be available. This proposition is, however, a useful base for sequential policy-making aimed at reducing the risks to democracy.[16]

Democratic governments everywhere face increasing challenge to the capacity to govern.[17] It suffices to mention nuclear confrontation, unemployment, stagflation, energy, ethnic politics, and environmental issues. Under such conditions, terrorism can cause grievous and even pivotal damage. In weakened democracies, the regime may change into a nondemocratic

15. A recent study on the downfall of the Weimar Republic shows that terrorism was more a symptom than a causal factor. See Karl Dietrich Erdmann and Hagen Schulze, eds., *Weimar: Selbstpreisgabe einer Demokratie—Eine Bilanz Heute* (Dusseldorf: Droste Verlag, 1980).

16. A full exposition of the problems of policy studies belongs to another occasion, but let me add three comments: (1) When dealing with long-range issues, such as the impact of terrorism on democracies, a long-term perspective is necessary, as illustrated for instance, by S. N. Eisenstadt in *The Political Systems of Empires: The Rise and Fall of the Historical Bureaucratic Societies* (Glencoe: Free Press, 1963). Policy-making cannot wait for historic perspectives, so that how to deduce the shape and variables of long-term processes from thin slices of time is a question to which there is no satisfactory answer. (2) The best of policy studies are doubtful when they deal with broad and complex issues such as terrorism. Policy-making and ways of reasoning must be adjusted to these features of inherently limited knowledge. Additional modes of policy reasoning must be added to those discussed in Stephen Toulmin, Richard Rieke, and Allan Janik, *An Introduction to Reasoning* (London: Collier Macmillan, 1979). (3) Knowledge for policy-making is useful on grounds of "preferability," in the sense that with the help of that knowledge, policy-making would be better off than without it. This criterion is different from that of most social science "public knowledge"; see J. M. Ziman, *Public Knowledge: An Essay Concerning the Social Dimensions of Science* (London: Cambridge University Press, 1968).

17. This subject is often termed "governability." See Michael J. Crozier, et al., *The Crisis of Democracy: Report on the Governability of Democracies to the Trilateral Commission* (New York: New York University Press, 1975); and Wilhelm Hennis, et al., eds., *Regierbarkeit* (Stuttgart: Klett-Cotta, vol. 1, 1977, vol. 2, 1979). I regard the concept "governability" as one-sided and prefer the term "capacity to govern." See Dror, *Public Policymaking Reexamined*. Cf. Robert L. Heilbroner, *Beyond Boom and Crash* (New York: Norton, 1978); and Arnold Brecht, *Kann die Demokratie überleben? Die Herausforderungen der Zukunft und die Regierungsformen der Gegenwart* (Stuttgart: Deutsche Verlags-Anstalt, 1978).

one, with terrorism serving as a convenient "enemy"[18] ostensibly justifying such a step. Democracy may perish inadvertently, as a consequence of shock effects, or because democratic institutions cannot treat decaying internal security.[19] In robust democracies, terrorism may aggravate preexisting government overloads,[20] reducing problem-handling capacity in general, distorting policy agendas, causing panic decisions, and increasing the opportunity costs caused by devoting scarce mental attention and capacities to terrorism. Terrorism may also exert a hidden influence on decisions; the impact of personal threats on decision-makers, for example, is not easy to discern.

Contemporary democracies are characterized by increasing levels of political tension, disconsensus, single-interest groups, true-belief movements, extraparliamentary militant action, and other tendencies that intensify conflict. Under such conditions, the thresholds between acceptable means of public pressure and illegitimate violence tend to erode. Combined with weakened government authority and legitimacy, on one hand, and ethnic tensions and economic depressions on the other, the potential for escalating violence grows. Here terrorism may cause its most extreme damage by further and dramatically breaking down the monopoly of government over violence and by eliminating inhibitions against the use of violence as a tool of politics. In a political culture becoming accustomed to terrorism, intensely committed groups may be socialized to consider violence an acceptable means of fighting for their values in the domestic arena. This solution violates the norms of working democracy and undermines liberalism.

Terrorism causes or reinforces analogous processes in international relations, breaking some of the few remaining restric-

18. The convenience of having enemies, as fully discussed by the German scholar Carl Schmitt, sometimes makes terrorism attractive for governments besieged by difficult domestic problems.
19. However distasteful, the advance design of "crisis regimes," sometimes called "constitutional dictatorships," can help assure the revival of democracies when they break under loads they cannot handle.
20. See Richard Rose, ed., *Challenge to Governance: Studies in Overloaded Polities* (Beverly Hills: Sage, 1980).

tions on "permissible" modes of violence and adding to the barbarization of the global system. Democracies are at a serious disadvantage, bound as they usually feel themselves to be by conventional and sometimes ill-fitting rules of international law.[21] Close connections between international political terrorism and what I call "crazy states"[22] combine to create situations hard to face without underreaction and perhaps subsequent overreaction. Terrorism contributes to the development of increasingly predatory and semibarbaric modes of international conflict, which democracies have difficulty in handling effectively.

Terrorism, together with other factors, has an important if abstract impact on the shape of future global culture and society. Hopes that democracy is the regime of the future and that authoritarianism is ephemeral are undermined by terrorism and by the apparent inability of democracies to obliterate it. The attractiveness of democracy for Third World countries is diminished by the spectacle of terrorism, which may help unmake democracy as the globally dominant form of regime and political culture, with sore consequences for the prosperity of humanity as a whole and for the future of democracy as a minority form of governance.

Let me be careful to avoid overstatement: terrorism is not the principal cause of deterioration in the domestic or the international reputation of democracies. Neither is the reduction of terrorism a key panacea for the ills of democracy.

Proposition No. 5. Terrorism imposes on limited capacities to govern and, especially, reinforces domestic and international tendencies toward unrestrained uses of violence. Distinctly dangerous are the undermining of weak democracies and the contribution to global neobarbarism.

21. There is no need to go to the extremes of Claire Sterling, *The Terror Network: The Secret War of International Terrorism* (New York: Reader's Digest Press/Holt, Rinehart, and Winston, 1981), to recognize that conventional legal thinking in democracies is slow to adjust to new needs. See the valuable but overconservative study by Alona E. Evans and John F. Murphy, eds., *Legal Aspects of International Terrorism* (Lexington, Mass.: D. C. Heath, 1978).

22. See Yehezkel Dror, *Crazy States: A Counterconventional Strategic Problem*, 2d ed. (Milwood, N.Y.: Kraus Reprint, 1980).

Future Perspectives

Any consideration of grand-policies for countering terrorism must be based on a view of its future shapes and costs, although reliable prediction is impossible, not only because suitable prediction methods are underdeveloped[23] but also because of the built-in indeterminacy of the phenomenon. The future of terrorism depends on stochastic and arbitrary (in the statistical sense) interconnections between a large number of dynamic and ultradynamic variables. For example, whether and how terrorism will escalate to unconventional weapons systems, such as toxic materials and nuclear devices, cannot be predicted, despite intense preoccupation with this horrifying possibility.[24] Subjective judgment and guesses are involved in all considerations of future perspectives of terrorism: this has important implications for handling uncertainty in counterterrorism decision-making.[25]

Pondering possible and probable futures of terrorism, I have in mind a short and medium time span, about five to twenty years, even though governments must learn to take into account long time spans in the range of fifty to one hundred years. We do not know whether terrorism is a temporary curse sure to weaken or whether over the long run it will develop into a major catastrophe. Yet, because of uncertainties and lim-

23. The best relevant collection includes little useful for our needs. See Nazli Choucri and Thomas W. Robinson, eds., *Forecasting in International Relations* (San Francisco: Freeman, 1978). Prediction methods for domestic situations are even less developed.

24. See Brian M. Jenkins, *Will Terrorists Go Nuclear?* (Santa Monica: Rand, 1975); Brian M. Jenkins, *The Potential for Nuclear Terrorism* (Santa Monica: Rand, 1977); and Robert Kuppermann and Darrell Trent, *Terrorism: Threat, Reality, Response* (Stanford: Hoover Institution Press, 1979), chapter 2.

25. The situation here, as in most difficult policy issues, is one of "fuzzy betting," where the choices are between various mixes of uncertainty and ignorance. The problem of terrorism can serve as a test of the utility of available methods in policy analysis, business problem solving, operations research, complexity management, and policy planning. Very little that is useful for analyzing problems like terrorism on a grand-policy level can be discerned, despite very intensive search of this literature. This finding in no way discounts the value of that literature for other purposes but reveals an urgent need to upgrade advanced policy analysis to be of real help to hard-pressed governments.

ited governmental capacities for handling long-term eventualities, only a short to medium time span for policy planning is feasible. Furthermore, policies toward terrorism should be reconsidered and revised according to changing conditions.[26]

With this perspective in mind, I can offer several possibilities for the future.[27] Nearly all conditions thought to breed terrorism will probably aggravate in the short and medium future. Value nihilism (in the technical sense of that term); the search for new beliefs, especially by the younger generation; disappointment with the established order; and broad public malaise will probably increase. Scarcities, unemployment, ethnic tensions, nuclear *Angst*, acute ecological problems, and the frustration of welfare aspirations are sure to increase in most democracies. Value cleavages and intense disconsensus, with groups strongly committed to contrary views, may well grow. International anarchism, hostilities, and fanaticism will expand. Poor Third World countries, well equipped with weapons but unable to handle their problems, will probably direct their hostility at democracies. The confrontation between communism and democracy will continue and perhaps escalate.

Technical tools for expanding terrorism and the vulnerability of democracies to terrorism will increase. Microtechnologies, biotechnologies, and nuclear technologies combine to produce knowledge and instruments highly suitable for esca-

26. Terrorism differs, for instance, from energy issues, where new and very long-range policies are necessary. See Wolf Hafele, *Energy in a Finite World: Paths to a Sustainable Future* (Cambridge, Mass.: Ballinger, 1981). Terrorism is far from being the most difficult issue faced by contemporary democracies either in content or in the policy-making modes necessary to handle it. An interesting approach, which may be applied to phased counterterror policy-making, is presented in C. S. Holling, ed., *Adaptive Environmental Assessment and Management* (New York: Wiley, IIASA Volume, 1980).

27. The following summary predictions are based on processed predictive literature, as illustrated by Thomas E. Jones, *Options for the Future: A Comparative Analysis of Policy-Oriented Forecasts* (New York: Praeger, 1980); and OECD, *Interfutures: Facing the Future—Mastering the Probable and Managing the Unpredictable* (Paris: OECD, 1979). My reading of the future is more pessimistic than the bulk of literature. Even a good study such as *Interfutures* ignores conflict, military activities, and terrorism. I suggest ignoring writings such as Alvin Toffler, *The Third Wave* (New York: Bantam, 1981, first published 1980) when trying to face the future seriously.

lating terrorism. At the same time, basic democratic freedoms will provide a convenient space for terrorism to operate in. Aging populations, additional leisure-time facilities, and continued urbanization will provide "soft" human targets. Modern energy facilities, data networks, roboted factories, and the like will add critical material targets. The ease of international communications and movements, mass-media attention to terrorism, and informal international networks that support terrorism constitute further trends that will permit or encourage terrorism.

Proposition No. 6. Known variables that breed and enable terrorism will increase in the near and medium future. Therefore, the expansion of terrorism is possible.

My choice of the term "possible" over "probable" is deliberate. In principle, I oppose the use of vague terms such as "probable" when the range of probabilities they are supposed to convey is not indicated.[28] Not enough is known about the factors that induce or inhibit terrorism to justify probabilistic predictions,[29] which should at least be limited to specific countries. I am also doubtful about so-called "surprise-free" predictions, which assume that the present will evolve linearly into the future. Terrorism is a turbulent affair, and surprises may occur, reshape reality, and change probabilities. To illustrate this point: unconventional terrorism could shock countries into radical action to eliminate terrorism; however, if no unconventional terrorism occurs within twenty years, this fact would require reconsideration of the prediction of future unconventional terrorism.

Since we are unable to establish probabilities for various expansions of terrorism, the formulation of comprehensive strat-

28. See Washington Platt, *Strategic Intelligence Production* (New York: Praeger, 1957), especially chapter 6, pp. 205–11, which, however simplistic, makes good sense on the need to specify degrees of certainty.

29. The use of subjective probabilities in such cases is misleading. For diverse approaches, see Howard Raiffa, *Decision Analysis: Introductory Lectures on Choices under Uncertainty* (Reading, Mass.: Addison, Wesley, 1968); and Amos Tversky and Daniel Kahneman, "Availability: A Heuristic for Judging Frequency and Probability," *Cognitive Psychology* 5 (1973): 207–32.

egies for counterterrorism must be adjusted to uncertainty. A phased learning approach should be adopted and policies developed sequentially, according to constantly reevaluated estimates of changing realities. The "principle of minimum regret" should serve as a decision criterion; it provides that being prepared for terrorism that does not occur is better than being unprepared for terrorism that does, even if its a priori probabilities are assumed to be low.[30]

Exploration of the possible dimensions of expanding terrorism may aid us in handling contingencies. We may see a quantitative growth of terrorism without changes in form; more of the same occurs in denser waves. There may be escalation in tools, with terrorists using advanced weapons technologies, such as toxic materials, remote control instruments, microtechnologies, or nuclear devices. Escalation in targets is possible, involving mass threats against urban concentrations, demonstration hits against cultural facilities, taking children as hostages, or action against scarce persons such as artists. The causes of terrorism may widen to embrace ecology, disarmament, religion, unemployment, and the like. Terrorist demands may raise the ante. Here I refer to a more determined terrorism, involving terrorists willing to take higher risks, and posing more extreme demands, such as shifts in national policies. Increased sophistication, with improvements in tactics, negotiations, and command and control is also possible; most terrorism has been weak in these matters.

We must consider combinations of these syndromes. Some growth in quantity is the least serious threat in most democracies. The most disturbing possiblity is a combination of

30. Unconventional terrorism belongs in part to the difficult category of very low probability and very high impact contingencies, along with nuclear war, earthquakes, or fatal diseases produced by genetic engineering. Analysis has only begun to face the mixture of psychological, logical, economic, mathematical, cultural, and other variables that shape the preferable responses to such possibilities. Seen against the background of many such contingencies, unconventional terrorism looks different than in isolation. Assuming that governmental capacities to prepare for such events are limited, the opportunity costs of contingency preparations for unconventional terrorism are very different from cost-benefit assessment.

widened causes, uniting far-reaching demands with sophistication and expansion of tools and targets. Such a possibility is very costly in itself. In addition, its negative impact on democracies may be multiplied by other domestic and international pressures.[31] The second-order consequences of terrorism may become more onerous. The possibility of expanded terrorism afflicting democracies during sensitive transition periods makes the improvement of strategies against terrorism an urgent task.

Proposition No. 7. Terrorism may escalate tools and targets, serve widened causes, raise demands, and become more sophisticated. If democracies are hit during difficult transition periods, the direct and indirect costs of terrorism may grow significantly.

"Report from Copper Mountain on Benefits of Terrorism"[32]

There is a devil's advocate position on these issues, the gist of which is that terrorism performs positive functions and that its containment and reduction may cause more harm than good. An imaginative book, *Report from Copper Mountain on Benefits of Terrorism,* might make the following points: (1) Terrorism serves as a safety vent for letting off dangerous pressures. Better to let this vent continue to function and even from time to time let terrorism succeed than to allow worse substitutes to develop should the forces presently causing terrorism be frustrated. Frustration and failure would also encourage the ex-

31. Without accepting all the conclusions of William Ophuls, *Ecology and the Politics of Scarcity: Prologue to a Political Theory of the Steady State* (San Francisco: Freeman, 1977), I think he and similar writers are correct in indicating that democracies will have to undergo difficult transformations, though probably not on the lines predicted by studies that neglect technology. Such transformation epochs, which may easily take a generation or two, create very awkward periods to face expanding terrorism. More misleading are the optimistic imaginings of Toffler or of Julian L. Simon, *The Ultimate Resource* (London: Martin Robertson, 1980).
32. Title and idea follow in the footsteps of Leonard C. Lewin (pseud.), *Report from Iron Mountain on the Possibility and Desirability of Peace* (New York: Delta, 1967).

pansion of terrorism. (2) Terrorism serves as a useful political drama, helping to maintain solidarity with the forces of law and order and to mobilize support for government. Therefore, terrorism helps rather than hinders the capacity to govern. (3) Terrorism keeps governments on the alert, preventing routinization and stimulating innovations and high energy efforts. Thus terrorism helps governments to learn at relatively low cost. (4) In the international arena, democracies should use rather than repress terrorism, to eliminate crazy rulers and inhibit antidemocratic forces. Other countries, in any case, will continue to employ terrorism, so why should not democracies teach the others a lesson in their own coin? If democracies do not want to dirty their own hands, they can always find proxies to act on their behalf. Indeed, carefully encouraging "freedom fighters" in antidemocratic countries may be a good way to destabilize them and prepare the ground for democratization.

The question of whether the total failure of terrorism in achieving any symbolic successes will reduce attempts at terrorism or will cause escalation to unconventional weapons is serious. The difficulty of deciding to let terrorism win from time to time, in order to reduce the motivation to escalate, adds to the problematics of designing and implementing appropriate comprehensive "grand-strategies."

Proposition No. 8. Terrorism is too complex an issue for handling through "common sense" and intuitive solutions once it expands beyond a domain where different treatments have approximately equivalent outcomes.[33]

33. I am returning here to a more complicated approach to evaluating the apparent success of most democracies in handling terrorism; it may be that, in the face of relatively limited terrorism and with suitable public relations, nearly all outcomes of counterterrorism decisions are more or less equally successful (or can at least be presented as such). For instance, if hostages are released when no ransom has been paid, then surely the policy was a success; if hostages are released after a ransom is paid, the government is credited with saving innocent lives; or if the hostages are murdered because no ransom is paid, the government claims to have stood firm and discouraged future hostage-taking. Only in cases such as military interventions are results clearly visible. Yet, ironically, results alone are not a reliable indicator of the wisdom of decisions to use force, because of "calculated risks." The apparent success of democracies in handling terrorism, therefore, does not permit far-reaching conclusions on their capacities to handle more difficult situations.

Governmental Capacities versus Terrorism

My conclusion that until now democracies as a whole have been successful in containing and handling terrorism poses serious problems for the development of novel grand-strategies against terrorism. We must face the questions of when governments should evolve and apply new grand-strategies and whether governments in fact are able and willing to do so.[34] As long as terrorism is limited and the damage it causes small, even taking negative second-order consequences into account, it may be better not to risk incorrect innovative interventions, which may cause more harm than good. It may be preferable to continue present policies, with incremental improvements. Such present policies as "playing down" and "population desensitization," followed successfully if unevenly by most democracies, are promising.

Historic and comparative studies, especially their pessimistic findings that the causes of governmental incapacities are built in and that the chances of present governmental machineries producing high-quality policies are low, reinforce this hesitation.[35] As long as disjointed incrementalism and other normal decision modes can reduce the need for high-quality

34. Here we run into another paradox, well illustrated by the terrorism issue, but going beyond it: when a problem is handled in what is perceived to be a satisfying way, there will be little propensity to engage in policy innovation. Therefore, in domains in which problems change rapidly and without warning and former government policies have been viewed as successful, a lag between new conditions and the continuing application of old policies is nearly unavoidable. Obvious failures of policies are also bad lessons, often resulting in entrenchment, dissonance-reducing defense moves, and/or panic learning. Limited failures may be the most conducive situation for policy innovation. It would be interesting to study government responses to terrorism within such theoretical frameworks, but studies of terrorism are divorced from organizational and governmental decision theory. For instance, governmental decisionmaking with respect to terrorism may permit reconsideration of important theories on governmental learning and on organizational behavior under conditions of uncertainty. See, respectively, Karl W. Deutsch, "On the Learning Capacity of Large Political Systems," in Manfred Kochen, ed., *Information for Action: From Knowledge to Wisdom* (New York: Academic Press, 1975), pp. 61–83; and James G. March, Johan P. Olsen, et al., *Ambiguity and Choice in Organizations* (Oslo: Universitetsforlagets, 1976).
35. This is the main thrust of my present research, *On the Incapacity to Govern.*

governmental grand-policies, such policies should be delayed. Since governments can expect an aggravation of policy predicaments and growing pressures on their capacities, requiring maximum effort, it is important that they keep as many problems as possible in the realm of ordinary or minimal-effort policy-making.

Recommendation A: As long as the costs of terrorism to democracies can be absorbed, no radical changes in counterterrorism policies should be introduced.

The dangers are that (1) in some democracies the costs of terrorism may already be too high, especially when second-order consequences are taken into consideration; (2) terrorism may expand and/or democracies may become more sensitive to terrorism, without early warning signs; and (3) development and implementation of adequate grand-strategies requires time, so that undertaking them after terrorism has visibly expanded and/or accelerated its damage may entail large costs. If we add the high probabilities of panic reactions to expanded terrorism, and if we apply the "principle of minimum regret," the following recommendation seems justified.

Recommendation B: Contingency preparation of counterterrorism grand-policies to face possible new situations should take place urgently, together with improved monitoring of trends and possible expansionist tendencies.

The monitoring requirement is not simple. Much intelligence work necessarily concentrates on already active terrorism. A major danger exists of new groups entering the field of terrorism, requiring an expansion of monitoring. The country may then face the dilemma of choosing between a police state and the shock of terrorism.

The requirement that grand-policies be prepared is difficult, because its political, moral, organizational, intellectual, and methodological requisites go beyond contemporary capabilities of most democracies. Methodologically and intellectually, terrorism is complex, partly indeterminate, and fuzzy. The issue is far beyond the domains of quantitative methods as well as contemporary social science approaches. A complexity-handling orientation must be combined with phased learning. The subjective knowledge and tacit skills of top-quality analysts, practitioners, and scholars are also necessary.[36] The development and implementation of new grand-policies cannot take place within existing organizational structures and politics. A separate "island of excellence" is probably required for developing grand-policy options, with final decision and implementation depending on intense involvement by rulers.[37] Some moral Gordian knots will have to be cut, with all the attendant anguish, disagreement, and dangers. The usual political processes of adjustment and compromise cannot achieve the nec-

36. The potential of quantitative analysis of counterterrorism measures is well illustrated in Hanan Alon, *Countering Palestinian Terrorism in Israel: Toward a Policy Analysis of Countermeasures* (Santa Monica: Rand, 1980). See also William W. Fowler, *An Agenda for Quantitative Research on Terrorism* (Santa Monica: Rand, 1980). Quantitative methods can only be a secondary tool in developing counterterrorism grand-policies. We need policy analysis knowledge that is more advanced than the state-of-the-art. At present, relevant skills exist to some extent in the minds of experienced people, but this is not enough of a base to meet policy-making needs. See Aaron Wildavsky's insightful *Speaking Truth to Power: The Art and Craft of Policy Analysis* (Boston: Little, Brown, 1979).

37. I use the concept "ruler" to refer to heads of governments and, in some parliamentary democracies, also one or two of the senior ministers. Rulers are crucial in achieving essential shifts in policies beyond incremental adjustment. U.S. political science underrates their pivotal function in social architecture; see Charles E. Lindblom, *The Intelligence of Democracy* (New York: Free Press, 1965); or Charles E. Lindblom and David K. Cohen, *Useable Knowledge: Social Science and Social Problem Solving* (New Haven: Yale University Press, 1979). Even the classic Richard E. Neustadt, *Presidential Power: The Politics of Leadership from FDR to Carter* (New York: Wiley, 1980, 1st ed., 1960) underestimates the capacity of a suitable president, with a well-equipped staff, to overcome political fragmentation and push through policy shifts. Recent U.S. experiences also contradict James L. Sundquist, "The Crisis of Competence in Government," in Joseph A. Pechman, ed., *Setting National Priorities: Agenda for the 1980's* (Washington, D.C.: The Brookings Institution, 1980), pp. 531–63. Valerie Bunce, *Do New Leaders Make a Difference: Executive Succession and Public Policy under Capitalism and Socialism* (Princeton: Princeton University Press, 1981); and, especially, Robert C. Tucker, *Politics as Leadership* (Columbia: University of Missouri Press, 1981), better recognize the essential functions of rulers under modern democratic conditions. Rulers must, however, be restrained; see Jon Elster, *Ulysses and the Sirens: Studies in Rationality and Irrationality* (New York: Cambridge University Press, 1979), chapter 2; and Yehezkel Dror, "Policy Analysis for Advising Rulers," forthcoming, and *Thinkbook for Rulers*, in preparation.

essary quality and consistency of policy, political will, or consensus. Much will depend on political leadership and entrepreneurship[38] and on political skills.[39]

Whereas "large-scale policy making"[40] is required for effective grand-strategies, fragmentary politics characterizes most democracies. Ad hoc adjustments to political situations and disjointed decisions by different power centers, interconnected by various bargaining modes, tend to dominate policy-making. Whether and how far counterterrorism grand-policy-making can be detached from the usual features of fragmented politics and located in enclaves of more compact, coherent, and consistent policy-making is an open question.

Reliance on crisis management to achieve effective policy-making is misplaced. Despite multiple ideas for improving crisis management,[41] few of them have been implemented. For example, crisis management doctrines require that top deci-

38. The possibility of an administrative entrepreneur "taking over" the subject is interesting but probably not realistic, given the hot political contents of terrorism. See Eugene Lewis, *Public Entrepreneurship: Towards a Theory of Bureaucratic Political Power—The Organizational Lives of Hyman Rickover, J. Edgar Hoover, and Robert Moss* (Bloomington: Indiana University Press, 1980).

39. See Robert E. Goodin, *Manipulatory Politics* (New Haven: Yale University Press, 1980). I argue that rulers should undertake important educational and political tasks in mobilizing support for necessary counterterrorism grand-strategies, as well as in using unavoidable terrorist incidents to strengthen thresholds against violence.

40. Paul R. Schulman, *Large-Scale Policy Making* (New York: Elsevier, 1980), is very important for reevaluating the requisites for adequate policy-making in different issue areas.

41. On the subject of crisis management, compare Ole R. Holsti, *Crisis Escalation War* (Montreal: McGill–Queen's University Press, 1972), Charles F. Hermann, ed., *International Crises: Insights from Behavioral Research* (New York: Free Press, 1972); Carolyn Smart and Ilan Vertinsky, "Design for Crisis Decision Units," *Administrative Science Quarterly* 22 (December 1977): 640–57; Margaret G. Hermann and Charles F. Hermann, "Maintaining the Quality of Decision Making in Foreign Policy Crisis: A Proposal," paper presented at the International Conference on Psychological Stress and Adjustment in Time of War and Peace, Tel Aviv, Israel, January 6–10, 1975; C. F. Smart and W. T. Stanbury, eds., *Studies in Crisis Management* (Toronto: Butterworth, Institute for Research in Public Policy Volumes, 1978); Michael Brecher, ed., *Studies in Crisis Behavior* (New Brunswick: Transaction Books, 1979); and Robert H. Kupperman, et al., "Crisis Management: Some Opportunities," in Kupperman and Trent, *Terrorism*, pp. 224–43.

sion-makers participate in crisis exercises, because in real incidents they will dominate choice; in reality, top politicians usually refuse to put themselves in artificial situations where their performance is subject to evaluation. Even very good crisis management is no substitute for appropriate counterterrorism grand-policies, although it is essential for applying policies and adjusting them to shifting situations.

Unavoidably, major counterterrorism policies will be implemented by decisions made in times of crisis. Immediate pressures and pragmatic considerations will dominate decisions, frequently displacing policy principles fully agreed to earlier. The divergences between actual policy-making characteristics and the requisites of counterterrorism grand-strategies lead me to the following conclusion.

Proposition No. 9. Preparation of adequate counterterrorism grand-policies and their implementation require extraordinary governmental and political arrangements and efforts.

Given this requirement, is terrorism worth the trouble? Should priority not be given to other issues in allocating very scarce high-quality policy-making capacities in governments? The concrete answer to this question depends on the circumstances of particular cases. The acuteness of the danger of terrorism as compared to other threats and the actual scarcity and opportunity costs of policy-making capacities are relevant. Perhaps policy options should be prepared outside the main arena of government. Think tanks could play important roles in this task.[42] In some cases, such work might be considered as a way to improve policy-making capacities that could later be used for more pressing issues. It might also be combined with the development of broad grand-policies for handling the basic syndromes of which terrorism is only one element.

The need for a broad-spectrum antidote is a principal conclu-

---

42. The contribution to counterterrorism policies of think tanks, such as the Rand Corporation or the Hudson Institute, is another subject that needs study. See Yehezkel Dror, "Think Tanks: A New Invention in Government," in Carol H. Weiss and Allen H. Barton, eds., *Making Bureaucracy Work* (Beverly Hills: Sage, 1980), pp. 139–52.

sion of my analysis. The worst damage of terrorism lies in its second-order consequences. Counterpolicies directed at them and at the syndrome behind them are the most cost-effective. We hope that expanded terrorism will not take place. If it does not, broad-spectrum policies could still be useful in handling other challenges. Taking into account our inadequate understanding of the causes of terrorism, our inability to predict its future, and the analytical and political difficulties of the subject, broad and robust approaches have a better chance of achieving counterterrorist goals than attempts at fine tuning would.

It is often effective, as well as intellectually and politically easier, however, to handle tactical aspects of terrorism and to establish and adopt minipolicies. Therefore, concomitantly with work on counterterrorism grand-policies, care must be taken not to neglect these simpler and more narrow-gauged antiterrorism measures, at least until grand-policies are sufficiently developed to permit testing.

This point justifies an explicit prescription:

Recommendation C: Development of counterterrorism grand-policies should take place along with focused and tactical counterterrorism activities and not as a substitute for them. Care must be taken to adjust the implementation of tactical measures to grand-policies.

This recommendation touches upon another and important problem of democratic government, the adjustment of implementation to policy. Where authority tends to be dispersed and action ad hoc, there is little use in developing even outstanding grand-policies unless policy implementation is redesigned.[43]

43. Historical study of attempts at policy innovations and their results leads to conclusions beyond contemporary literature on "implementation." The lesson that innovative policies require radical changes in organizations is particularly relevant. See Daniel T. Orlovsky, *The Limits of Reform: The Ministry of Internal Affairs in Imperial Russia, 1802–1881* (Cambridge, Mass.: Harvard University Press, 1981). In a number of countries the need to set up special counterterror elite units illustrates this principle in action. See Roger A. Baumont, *Military Elites* (London: Robert Hale, 1974); and Eliot A. Cohen, *Commandos and Politicians: Elite Military Units in Modern Democracies* (Cambridge, Mass.: Harvard University Center for International Affairs, 1978).

Recommendation D: Implementation institutions have to be redesigned to increase the impact of counterterrorism grand-policies on actual events.
My principal conclusions on the desirable scope, loci, and integration of decisions are as follows.

Recommendation E: The preparation of counterterrorism options should be integrated with broader treatment of the syndromes of which terrorism is only a part.

Recommendation F: Relevant work should take place, in part, in think-tank units, with arrangements for the involvement of top decision-makers and for integration of think-tank findings into actual policy-making, including crisis decisions.

Recommendation G: Work on counterterrorism grand-policies should serve to improve the quality of general policy development.

Independent of these recommendations, I wish to emphasize the essential role of rulers in such decisions. Without their direct involvement, even if limited by time, there is little hope for approval from the top and none for implementation. Similarly, without suitable rehearsal in crisis management for senior participants, the heat of terrorist incidents will drive previously prepared policies out of their minds.

Recommendation H: Rulers and their staffs must be involved in the development and approval of policies toward terrorism.

Recommendation I: Crisis management must be specially prepared to increase the influence of approved grand-policies on actual crisis decisions.

Underlying these recommendations is a more general one, concerning the political climate and culture in which decisions take place. Leaving aside obvious exhortations on the need for creativity, an open mind, and so forth, I must point out the need to preserve a "cool" attitude of clinical concern in the face of overwhelming pressure and the heartbreaking impact of

---

Rigidities of juridical, political, and organizational structures inhibit implementation of innovative counterterrorism grand-policies.

tragic choices. Emotional considerations must not be permitted to dominate responsible policy-making.[44]

Recommendation J: Counterterrorism policy-making in all its modes requires protection against emotional overloads, panic effects, and the impact of strain and stress. Neglect of this problem characterizes much writing on how to handle terrorism, probably because the authors have inadequate experience with real high-level decision-making. How to guard against psychological errors depends on the conditions of specific countries; organization design and staff preparation must be tailor-made. Realization of this problem and of its acute impact on responses to terrorism is a sine qua non for the advancement of the other recommendations I have presented.

Toward Counterterrorism Grand-Policies

Most of my prescriptive treatment has been on a metapolicy level, that is, policy-making on how to make policy.[45] Nevertheless, let me conclude by presenting some concrete, if preliminary, illustrations to operationalize the concept of "grand-policy," to draw substantive conclusions from my analysis, and to clarify the propositions and recommendations I have made. These illustrations present difficult grand-policy decisions with high costs in social values, political consensus, individual rights, and international order. They also require massive effort and involve activities usually dispersed among several administrative agencies and sometimes located in private organizations.

Recommendation K: As an aid in reconsidering the general propositions and recommendations presented here, and as

44. Relevant in principle, though needing adjustment to fit complex decision-making situations, is Irving L. Janis and Leon Mann, *Decision Making: A Psychological Analysis of Conflict, Choice, and Commitment* (New York: Free Press, 1977).

45. See Dror, *Public Policymaking Reexamined.* The development of adequate policies to counter terrorism depends on upgrading present government capacities. The handling of terrorism can serve as a valuable case from which much can be learned on a variety of social science and policy science subjects. Little has been done to use this potential.

partial starting points for actual work on designing and developing the response to terrorism, the following grand-policies are proposed for consideration: (1) The monopoly of democratic governments over the use of violence should be reasserted, with strict thresholds established against shortcutting democratic political processes through militant action. Building additional barriers against the growing use of violence as a political tool should accompany the design of new ways, such as decentralization and referendums, for expressing opinions and demands.[46] (2) The support other governments provide for terrorism should be regarded as acts of aggression, justifying counterattacks, abolition of diplomatic immunities, and similar steps. Such reactions should be semiautomatic, following quasi-judicial procedures against such countries in an intergovernmental tribunal on crimes of terrorism to be set up unilaterally by the democracies. (3) Access to knowledge and materials that confer a potential for mass killing should be strictly controlled; no "right to learn or to teach" is acceptable with respect to extremely lethal information and skills. (4) Public counterterrorism policies should be strictly enforced, with private corporations and individuals bound to refuse payment of ransom or negotiations with hostage-takers if such steps are counter to promulgated public policy. (5) Symbolic awards to terrorists, such as the mass-media treatment of former terrorists as heroes, should be inhibited.

These are tentative ideas to be prepared for action if and when signs of expanding terrorism justify the effort and the

46. This proposal hints at the need to restructure institutions of democracy to meet changing problems and conditions. Simple solutions will not do. Thus the uses and misuse of referendums require careful study to design a mechanism, the advantages of which outweigh the disadvantages, that might, in conjunction with other steps, be part of a broad strategy to reduce violence as well as contain terrorism. See David Butler and Austin Ranney, eds., *Referendums: A Comparative Study of Practice and Theory* (Washington, D.C.: American Enterprise Institute, 1978); Austin Ranney, ed., *The Referendum Device* (Washington, D.C.: American Enterprise Institute, 1981); and Klaus G. Troitzsch, *Volksbegehren und Volksentscheid: Eine vergleichende Analyse direktdemokratischer Verfassungsinstitutionen unter besonderer Berücksichtigung der Bundesrepublik Deutschland under der Schweiz* (Königstein/Ts.: Athenäum, 1979).

moral and political costs. Implementation should, if possible, be in stages so as to inhibit the expansion of terrorism and avoid premature or tardy counteraction.

Realistic Prospects

Some of the facts considered here make it unlikely that democracies will develop and implement the proposed grand-strategies against terrorism. Apparent success in handling present terrorism with limited innovations in policy-making; overloads of more pressing issues; political, organizational, moral, and intellectual costs and difficulties of evolving grand-strategies; and general incapacity to engage diffuse and futuristic problems that deviate from dominant policy mind-sets—all these combine to reduce the probability of rapid progress.

This conclusion comes as no surprise. It is the tension between the limited capacities for response inherent in democratic government and the crises posed by harsher challenges that constitutes the most important issue I have examined here. A possible lesson from the analysis of "terrorism and democracy" goes far beyond the subject itself: we need to take a skeptical look at democratic capacities to govern and to upgrade them with haste. This implication, if correct, may be critical for the survival and the viability of democracy in an increasingly demanding, if not neobarbaric, world.

Conor Cruise O'Brien

5

Terrorism
under Democratic Conditions:
The Case of the IRA

The words "terrorism" and "terrorist" are not terms of scientific classification. They are imprecise and emotive. We do not apply them to all acts of politically motivated violence nor to all people who commit such acts. We reserve their use, in practice, for politically motivated violence *of which we disapprove.* The words imply a judgment—sometimes a very complex judgment—about the political context in which those whom we decide to call terrorists operate, and above all a judgment about the nature of the regime under which and against which they operate. We imply that that regime itself is *legitimate.* If we call them "freedom fighters" we imply that the regime is *illegitimate.* If we call them *"guerrillas"* we may not be quite sure what we ought to think about the *regime;* we imply at the least that we wish to distance ourselves from the regime.

Very few of us would use the word "terrorist" as a general description of members of the Resistance during the Nazi occupation of France. If members of Solidarity today in Poland began to shoot members of the security police, few in the West

would call them terrorists. And some of us—I included—
would refuse to apply the label "terrorist" to persons who use
political violence for the overthrow of the regimes in, for example, El Salvador, Guatemala, and South Africa.

I would not call such people "freedom fighters" either. That
is a label with which one should be very sparing. We do not
know whether they are really freedom fighters until they win
power. Joseph Stalin and Pol Pot may have appeared to be freedom fighters when they were in opposition to the regime, but
when they won power they allowed no freedom. They simply
practiced, on a far greater scale, the same crafts of violence and
intimidation—terror—they had used in opposition, allegedly
in the cause of freedom. Even some we might think of as the
most incontestable freedom fighters—the French Resistance—
behaved toward the population of Madagascar and Algeria very
much as the Nazis behaved in France, as was clearly foreseen
by Simone Weil when she was working with the Free French in
London.

In *L'Enracinement* she referred to the possible danger that
the Free French movement might turn into something fascist
for fascism was always intimately connected with a certain pa-
triotic feeling. As regards the Free French and the empire, she
wrote: "It may be that France now has to choose between her
attachment to her Empire and the need to have a soul of her
own again. . . . If she chooses wrongly, if we ourselves force her
to choose wrongly, which is only too likely, she will have
neither the one nor the other, but only the most appalling
adversity."[1]

The terms "terrorist" and "freedom fighter," then, are slippery. They will go on being slippery, in general use, because
they are banner words, fighting words, never purely descriptive. They are of course used differently on the left and on the
right. The left is suspicious of "terrorist" and lavish with "freedom fighter" and similar terms when applied to people who
fight against right-wing regimes in the Third World. The right

---

1. (Paris: Gallimard, 1949), p. 146; see also p. 129. Translation mine.

is more systematic: for them people who use political violence under communist regimes are freedom fighters; those who use political violence under noncommunist and anticommunist regimes are terrorists.

Is there any way to escape such depressingly polemical usage? In one sense, no. In political and ideological struggles, words are weapons, not analytical tools. That has always been so. Nonetheless, it is possible to limit our own uses of the term "terrorism" and to apply it consistently and intelligibly, not as a mere war cry. Explicit adoption of criteria applicable in all cases is required. The criteria I suggest are those of *consent* and *participation*.

The basic criterion is *consent*. Where democracy, the rule of law, and freedom of expression exist there is, generally speaking, consent of the governed. Political and legal change is possible, also by consent. Where grievances exist, as they will, they can always be articulated and often mitigated. I would restrict the application of the word "terrorist" to one who, under these conditions, uses lethal violence to bring about political change.

So used, the term remains normative, indeed stigmatizing. It expresses a value judgment and a political judgment. Democracy, the rule of law, and so on are assumed to constitute a precious and useful inheritance, conducive to decent and civilized living. This is the value judgment. The political judgment is that the overthrow of democratic government, or serious encroachment on democracy, as a result of politically motivated violence, would constitute a grave setback to civilization and decency. So holding, we have coherent grounds for stigmatizing people who use political violence under democratic conditions as terrorists and for repressing terrorism by the enforcement of the law.

That is the criterion of consent. But democracy is not perfect; there are gray areas, borderline cases—often literally concerned with borders. To minorities who feel themselves to be in the wrong place, under a form of government they reject, it seems small enough consolation to be told that they belong to a democracy. If those who are ill-disposed to us are in a major-

ity, democracy is not, on the face of it, an attractive proposition.
And democratic governments have often discriminated against
minorities.

Under these conditions, should we regard the use of political
violence on behalf of a minority as terrorism, or should we be
inclined to see in it the legitimate revolt of people governed
without their consent—and so withhold the stigmatizing epithet? That is not an academic or hair-splitting question, though
it may sound as if it is. The success or failure of political violence depends very largely on the extent to which it is perceived as legitimate. The use of the designation "terrorism"
constitutes a declaration of the illegitimacy of the political violence referred to. So whether we use the term, refrain from
using it, or hesitate to use it has a bearing on how long the
political violence is likely to continue and how many lives it
will cost.

It is in connection with this question of the legitimacy of
political violence on behalf of a minority that I propose the
criterion of *participation*. If a minority is denied all participation in democratic process, other than that of voting and being
automatically outvoted, if it is denied the benefit of freedom of
expression and the rule of law, and thus deprived of any peaceful means of improving its situation, then it seems to me that it
would be inappropriate to describe as terrorists those who
might use political violence on behalf of such a minority. They
are in a position closely comparable to the subjects of arbitrary
power.

On the other hand, if a minority, in addition to being allo-
cated its due proportion of seats in parliament, enjoys the benefits of freedom of expression and the rule of law, then I would
not hesitate to describe as terrorists any persons who might
resort to political violence on behalf of such a minority. They
would still be terrorists, in my view, even if the minority on
whose behalf they act—or claim to act—are subject to serious
social disabilities. They would still be terrorists—their actions
would be illegitimate—because such a minority has access to

levers of peaceful change through the law and through the media.

Take the example of blacks in the southern states in the first half of this century. They were very nearly in the position of the first kind of minority I described. Their access to democracy was almost nonexistent; they were prevented from voting by force and by fraud; the interpretation and the enforcement of the law were in the hands of their enemies: systematic intimidation curbed their freedom of expression. In these conditions I could not have described as terrorists any blacks in the states of Mississippi or Alabama who might have resorted to violence against a system that virtually denied their humanity.

Yet as we all know, it was not through political violence that political change to the benefit of that minority was brought about. It was brought about by democratic processes: by the nonviolent civil rights movement, by media publicity and the pressure of public opinion, by the U.S. Supreme Court's interpretation of the Constitution, and by the political clout of enfranchised northern blacks and of whites who rejected southern law enforcement as they saw it on their television screens. All these forces are effective under democratic conditions and not under any others.

Southern blacks were the most politically—and otherwise— disadvantaged and deprived minority that has existed in any democracy in modern times. If their political disadvantages could be largely removed by democratic process, it is hard to see any good case for political violence on behalf of minorities less disadvantaged.

I would conclude that the use of violence for political ends within democratic societies should always be classified as terrorism and dealt with as such.

Against this general background, I should like to discuss the Provisional IRA, the longest-established organization of political violence operating within a democratic framework, or rather, democratic frameworks.

First, within the definitions I have proposed, the Provisional

IRA is unmistakably a terrorist organization. I so regard it and hold that it should be so treated. It should be dealt with by the enforcement of the law against its illegal activities and not by political negotiation in relation to its professed political aims.

Most of my fellow countrymen, however, would be reluctant, in varying degrees, to use the word "terrorist" in speaking about the IRA. Only a small minority supports the IRA and a majority condemns it. Yet even among that condemning majority, most would hesitate to describe the IRA as terrorists. That hesitation, still persisting after more than ten years of terror, is highly significant and ominous. It reflects a general ambivalence that contains, along with revulsion for its deeds, a kind of collusion, in the shape of an unwillingness to reject the IRA's credentials and deny its legitimacy.

This historically rooted ambivalence has enabled the IRA to wage, in Claire Sterling's words, "the longest war" of its kind.[2] Those who condemn it—or, more usually, its most recent spectacular act of lethal violence—are apt, more or less in the same breath, to accord its members the status of "misguided idealists," to endorse their objective—a united Ireland—and even to claim that the attainment of that objective is a necessary precondition for the ending of political violence. The IRA can also count on the support of many from this large ambivalent section for the nonviolent—propagandist—phases and aspects of its activity, such as hunger strikes, protests against prison conditions, and allegations of police brutality.

The ambivalent are important because they are numerous, central, and respectable. But the minority that gives varying levels of support with no more than limited reservations is also significant—not much less than 20 percent of the population in the Republic and possibly more than that as a proportion of the Catholic minority in Northern Ireland. The ambivalent and the vaguely supportive between them may make up more than half the Catholic population of the island of Ireland, although

2. *The Terror Network: The Secret War of International Terrorism* (New York: Reader's Digest Press/Holt, Rinehart, and Winston, 1981), chapter 9.

those who unequivocally support the IRA are a tiny minority. The IRA of course also draws on significant support from overseas, especially from America. All this makes up a political culture that is sustaining to this particular form of terrorism. In terms of Chairman Mao's famous metaphor, there is water enough for the fish.

The political movement of which the Provisional IRA is part is more than a hundred years old. It began in 1858 as the Irish Republican Brotherhood (IRB). Its American wing, known as Clan na Gael and as the Fenians, became especially important after the American Civil War. The IRB's objective was complete separation of Ireland from Britain, a separation to be obtained by physical force. Its military activities during the nineteenth century were sparse and futile, but the influence of its members—and especially former members—was significant to the development of Irish nationalism, though mainstream nationalism long remained constitutional and opposed to physical force.

The outbreak of World War I brought the IRB and its ideology into the mainstream of Irish history. In accordance with the revolutionary dictum "England's difficulty is Ireland's opportunity," the IRB decided on an insurrection with help from Germany. The planning was entrusted to the seven-member Military Council of the IRB, which decided on, planned, and led the Easter Rising of 1916. The seven members of the Military Council were also the signatories of the Proclamation of the Republic.

Militarily, the rising was a failure, crushed within a week. It received very little popular support. But the execution by the British of the leaders of the rising caused a widespread revulsion, intensified by a subsequent attempt to impose conscription in Ireland. The Sinn Fein party, professing allegiance to the Republic, won almost all the seats in Catholic Ireland in the general election of November 1918. But the same election showed—as had every election since the advent of universal suffrage—that in Eastern Ulster (what is now Northern Ireland) the Protestant majority rejected the Republic, preferring to remain in the United Kingdom.

The Sinn Fein representatives declined to attend the Parliament at Westminster, to which they had been elected, and met in Dublin, claiming to be the Parliament of all Ireland, Dail Eireann. The representatives of what is now Northern Ireland of course declined to attend this Parliament.

Armed forces acknowledging, in theory at least, the authority of Dail Eireann, began hostilities against the police and the British army. These forces were known as the Irish Republican Army. There followed some years of conflict between the IRA and British forces in a number of areas of Catholic Ireland, together with intercommunal fighting between Catholic and Protestant in what is now Northern Ireland. In December 1921, representatives of Dail Eireann signed a treaty with Great Britain by which Britain accepted the autonomy of the area that is now the Republic, and representatives of the Dail accepted that those areas—effectively, what is now Northern Ireland—in which an overall majority did not wish to join the Republic could remain in the United Kingdom.

A majority in Dail Eireann, and a majority of the people of the Republic, accepted the treaty. A minority in the Dail, and a part of the IRA, rejected the treaty, and there followed the Irish civil war of 1922–23. The pro-treaty forces won, but ten years later, Eamon de Valera, leader of the Dail minority that had rejected the treaty, came to power through free elections. De Valera's party, Fianna Fail, is still the largest party in the Republic.

Although de Valera, in entering the Parliament of the new state, accepted de facto what he had once opposed, a section of the armed forces that had fought against the treaty settlement continued to hold out against it, denying the legitimacy of both Northern Ireland and the twenty-six-county Republic and professing allegiance to the Republic proclaimed in 1916, for all Ireland, totally separate from Britain. This section is the IRA, and it has been in continuous existence, with varying degrees and phases of activity, in both the Republic and Northern Ireland over the past sixty years.

The IRA owes its remarkable durability to a variety of circumstances. As far as the Republic is concerned, the official rhetoric and symbolism of the state, based on the cult of the 1916 Easter Rising, have helped immeasurably. When the IRA and its friends point out that the existing Republic of twenty-six counties is not the Republic proclaimed in 1916, the democratic parties have no effective answer. And when the IRA is told it has no democratic mandate to wage war—as of course it does not—its spokesmen ask what democratic mandate the men of 1916 had. To that, there is no effective answer either. All this gives the IRA the credibility that belongs to people who act in accordance with ideals to which most people merely pay lip service.

As far as Northern Ireland is concerned, the main contribution comes from the sense of grievance of the substantial Catholic minority—more than a third of the population. From 1920 to 1972, Northern Ireland had a parliament with powers devolved to it from Westminster. In a society in which politics are polarized along sectarian lines, this meant that power was permanently in the hands of representatives of the Protestant majority. Because they regarded the Catholic minority as a threat to the existence of Northern Ireland, they used such powers as they possessed to the disadvantage of that minority, discriminating against them in relation to jobs, housing, and local government franchise.

The civil rights movement that arose in the late 1960s imitated the civil rights movement in the American southern states, seeking to do for Catholics what the American movement had done for blacks. To some extent, it was successful. It publicized the grievances of the Catholic minority, and the violent reactions it evoked from the police controlled by the Protestant majority aroused the sympathy of the British public in a way comparable to the reactions of the American North to reports from Dixie in the early 1960s. This reaction led to the deployment of British troops for the protection of the Catholic minority in August 1969; to the curbing of the powers of the Northern Ireland parliament—Stormont—and eventually, in 1972, to the abolition of that parliament. Since that date Northern Ireland has been under direct rule, and official discrimination against Catholics is at an end. As far as state responsibilities are concerned, the objectives of the civil rights movement have been attained.

The violence, however, has not ended or greatly lessened. The IRA remains firmly ensconced in the Catholic ghettos. The Provisional IRA—a nationalist breakaway from the old Marxist-led IRA, now known as the Officials—established itself solidly in the ghettos in 1969–70, being seen by many as a kind of Catholic defensive militia against Protestant violence. The Provisional IRA is not, however, a purely defensive body. Its object is to bring about a united Ireland totally separate from Britain. This objective is to be won by sustained terror, wearing down both the British will to remain in Northern Ireland and the will of Ulster Protestants to remain in the United Kingdom. In the first objective, the IRA may be meeting with some success. Certainly many people in Britain, including some prominent politicians, would like to disengage from Northern Ireland. Polls regularly show a majority—though not recently an increasing one—in favor of that course. There is a strong tendency in that direction in the Labour party, and some leading figures in the other parties are believed to incline in the same direction, as are some senior officials in the Foreign Office. The second objective has met with a peculiar kind of negative success. Evidence of a British trend toward disengagement inclines many Ulster Protestants toward some variety of independent Northern Ireland. This would not be a move toward a united Ireland—quite the contrary. An independent Northern Ireland, with of course its Protestant majority, would be a much less healthy environment for Northern Ireland's Catholics than the old Stormont of devolved powers ever was.

In the early 1970s it was possible to hope that Northern Catholics, having accepted the IRA in the role of defender, would turn against it when they realized the dangers and hardships being brought on Catholics as well as Protestants by the IRA's aggressive policies. There have been periods when it appeared that this would occur, but no decisive movement has yet emerged for several reasons. One of the strongest is a sinister piece of social dynamics: the greater the degree of anti-Catholic rage aroused in Protestant Ulster by the aggressive activities conducted by the IRA out of the Catholic ghettos, the greater the need felt for the IRA as armed defender of the ghettos against attack. Its aggression gives it an indispensable role in defense.

Another strong reason for the IRA's durability is the position of the Republic with its cult of the 1916 Rising and its insistence—loudly supported by Irish-Americans—that unification, the IRA's objective, is the inevitable and the only acceptable outcome. The two together suggest that the IRA is both legitimate and an eventual winner. These concepts pour more fuel on the ancient intercommunal hostilities of Northern Ireland, and the more fuel, the more the IRA benefits.

These, I believe, are the main reasons why the IRA has proved so durable. They leave us few grounds for hope that its campaign will soon be ended. That it will achieve its objective—a united Ireland—is even less likely. After all these years of murder, the Ulster Protestant majority are, if anything, less inclined than ever to accept a united Ireland. There is simply no way of including them in such an entity in this century or well into the next.

The only major change that is possible—and seems more likely now than it did some years ago—is British withdrawal, followed, not by a united Ireland but by an independent Northern Ireland in which security would be in the hands of the Protestant majority. Security would be the overriding concern of the authorities, and security policy would be directed toward flushing the IRA out of the Catholic ghettos. Granted the pathological nature of intercommunal relations in Northern Ireland, an attempt by Protestant forces to flush the IRA out of Catholic ghettos would precipitate civil war in Ireland.

Thus the only major change that is actually possible is one

that would make matters far worse than even their present bad condition. It seems preferable—though far from heartwarming—to continue with the essentials of the present situation, in the grim knowledge of the probability that "the longest war" will get even longer. That bleak conclusion is unpalatable to many, but the forbidding realities of the situation constrain me to it.

All my emphasis has been laid on the indigenous reasons for the durability of the war. I have not discussed the hypothesis suggested by Claire Sterling and others, including a few in Northern Ireland, that the IRA functions as part of an international conspiracy. I believe that hypothesis to be fanciful and misleading.[3] The Provisional IRA has occasionally used left-wing rhetoric, especially when engaged in exchange of technical information with (and collecting money or arms from) European and Arab terrorists. But basically it is an outgrowth of the deep-rooted ultranationalist physical-force tradition within the Irish Catholic (and nationalist) community. It is a thoroughly and bitterly native phenomenon, and no one who has studied it closely believes in the reality, or even the possibility, of its falling under foreign control.

Since the above essay was prepared, prospects of winding down violence in Northern Ireland have seemed in some ways to improve. The force behind this change is a deterioration in relationships between the IRA and the Catholic community out of which it operates, apparently as a result of the circumstances in which the IRA hunger strikes came to an end.

During the hunger strikes, through most of 1981, the IRA benefited from widespread Catholic sympathy reflected in large attendance at funerals; in the election of the IRA hunger striker Bobby Sands as MP for Fermanagh–South Tyrone; in the election of the pro-IRA candidate Owen Carron as his successor; and in vast publicity and money contributed.

In this period the IRA leadership persistently denied that it was orchestrating the hunger strikes. It claimed that the pris-

3. See my review of *The Terror Network* in *The New Republic*, July 25, 1981.

oners themselves had spontaneously gone on hunger strikes and that the decision as to whether or not to continue rested entirely with the prisoners. This view was widely accepted among the large Catholic public, which sympathized with the hunger strikers. Although sympathy was never as strong in the Republic as in the Catholic areas of Northern Ireland, two "H-Block" candidates (standing on the single issue of support for the hunger strikers) were elected to the Dail in the Republic's general elections of June 1981.

By the time of the death of the tenth hunger striker (Michael Devine) on August 20, it became apparent that the relatives of the surviving IRA prisoners wanted the hunger strikes called off, that members of the Catholic clergy were encouraging the relatives toward this end, and that the prisoners themselves were moving in that direction. It also became apparent that the IRA leadership very much wanted the hunger strikes to continue, notching up more deaths.

When the hunger strike was in fact brought to an end on October 3, 1981, the IRA leaders vented their frustration in bitter denunciations of the Catholic clergy for helping to bring this about. In particular, they attacked the Catholic prison chaplain, Fr. Denis Faul, a priest who was well-known—or notorious—for his vocal sympathy with their cause, but whose offense was that he had helped to save the lives of IRA prisoners whose deaths the IRA leaders believed would have been profitable to the cause. The IRA leaders also denounced the Catholic clergy in general and the hierarchy in particular.

This reaction seems to have caused a widespread reaction against the IRA among those who had rallied to its "humanitarian" cause in the early days of the hunger strikes. Certainly the Catholic clergy now became more explicit and businesslike in its opposition to the IRA. The bishop of Derry, Dr. Daly, told his congregation, after an IRA murder outside his cathedral, that it was their duty to cooperate with the police in the apprehension of murderers. He thus broke the old taboo against "informing," an important step. In the March elections in the

Republic a number of Sinn Fein candidates stood. All were heavily defeated, and the two H-Block seats were lost.

The circumstances in which the hunger strikes came to an end seem also to have had damaging effects inside the IRA. The IRA draws most of its active membership from a limited number of families, whose members know one another intimately. The traumatic events of the hunger-strike period are bound to leave a bitter legacy. It is probably significant that the anniversary (May 7) of the death of Bobby Sands passed very quietly; the commemoration was minimal by IRA standards and pathetic in comparison with the great outburst of mass emotion at the time of the death itself.

The Provisional IRA is still in business—still killing people—and there is no question of writing it off. There have been many ups and downs since it came into existence more than twelve years ago, and the present "down" may represent only a temporary setback. But this postscript is necessary to register that there are reasons to feel less pessimistic than I felt when writing my basic paper about the possibility of the IRA becoming more isolated from the community that has harbored it. The "water" just now looks distinctly less healthy for those "fish" in May 1982.

Paul Wilkinson

6

The Orange and the Green: Extremism in Northern Ireland

The latest phase of violent conflict in Northern Ireland has been going on since 1969. By May 1982 more than 2,200 people had died as a result of the most prolonged and severe terrorist campaign experienced in any West European democracy since 1945.[1] Total deaths through terrorism in the province in 1981, the year of the Maze hunger strike, reached 101, a 33 percent increase over the toll for 1980. Nor does there seem to be any immediate prospect of terrorism abating: total deaths through terrorism, including civilians, actually increased in the first quarter of 1982 compared to 1981.

It is against this background that James Prior's brave but cautious project[2] to establish "rolling devolution" in the province has to be seen. It appears that the British cabinet has now given

1. For recent discussions of terrorism in Northern Ireland see Paul Wilkinson, *Terrorism and the Liberal State* (New York: Wiley, 1977), pp. 86–92 and 150–70; J. Bowyer Bell, *A Time of Terror: How Democratic Societies Respond to Revolutionary Violence* (New York: Basic Books, 1978), pp. 204–33; and Frank Wright, "The Ulster Spectrum," in David Carlton and Carlo Schaerf, eds., *Contemporary Terror* (London: Macmillan, 1981).

2. Prior has been secretary of state for Northern Ireland since September, 1981. See Great Britain, *Northern Ireland: A Framework for Devolution*, Cmnd. 8541 (London: HMSO, 1982).

lukewarm support to Prior's plan to hold elections by the single transferable vote system of proportional representation for a seventy-eight member assembly. The White Paper envisages that in the initial phase the assembly would have scrutinizing, deliberative, and consultative functions and would be asked to recommend to the secretary of state arrangements under which the whole or part of the range of legislative and executive responsibilities could be exercised by the assembly and by a devolved administration answerable to it. Considerable flexibility is built in to the proposals, as reflected in the decision to proceed in stages and to leave the precise extent and nature of any devolved powers open for future decision. The White Paper refers to the possibility of either devolution en bloc or partial devolution under which only functions relating to specified Northern Ireland departments would be devolved, leaving others subject to direct rule.

There is also an imaginative degree of flexibility implicit in the process leading up to any transfer of powers. The secretary of state would be required to lay before Parliament any proposed scheme of devolution that had the support of 70 percent or more of the assembly. But it would also be open to him to invite the assembly to submit a scheme agreed to by a majority of less than 70 percent of the members of the assembly, provided it had sufficient cross-community support.[3]

It is very important not to set too great a store on the success of such a scheme in reaching an agreed form of devolved government. The wreckage of all previous attempts since 1972[4] is a bleak reminder of the difficulty of the task. Prior's scheme has received a clear welcome from only one Northern Ireland

3. Ibid., Part 5: "The Constitutional Proposals."
4. For example, the Northern Ireland Executive, which took office in January 1974, was formed in accordance with the Northern Ireland Constitution Act, 1973. The collapse of the Executive was followed by the Northern Ireland Act of 1974, which introduced temporary arrangements for direct rule. There was an attempt in 1975, through the Northern Ireland Constitutional Convention, to find a new system of devolved government acceptable to both communities, but its report was not found acceptable to Parliament. A further unsuccessful attempt was made at a 1980 constitutional conference convened by the secretary of state.

political party, the nonsectarian Alliance party. And it is distinctly ominous that the plan has already been firmly rejected by John Hume and his colleagues in the Social Democratic and Labour party, the major constitutional party representing the Catholic minority, and by Charles Haughey, prime minister of the Republic of Ireland, as "unworkable."

In addition, there is a small band of diehard "integrationists," a group of backbench Tory and Official Unionist MPs, who see even the most cautious move toward a power-sharing devolved government for Ulster as a sure sign of the British government's ultimate readiness to sever the union between the Loyalist Protestants and the United Kingdom. These integrationists regard any scheme for devolution as a sop to Republican extremism and violence that will only lead to more terrorism. Pointing out that Sir Edward Carson, the founding father of modern Ulster, was opposed to the establishment of a separate parliament in Northern Ireland,[5] they argue that it is a logical absurdity to introduce devolution for Ulster while Scotland and Wales remain undevolved.[6] The integrationists completely discount the fact that the province of Northern Ireland enjoyed fifty years of domestic autonomy between 1922 and the suspension of Stormont. This separate development led to the formation of a political culture, political parties, and methods of policy-making and administration unique to Northern Ireland.[7] Moreover, they conveniently overlook the fact that Ulster politics are different from those in the rest of the United Kingdom, above all because of the special problems inherent in the divisions between the majority and minority communities.

5. Edward Marjoribanks and Ian Colvin, *The Life of Lord Carson* (vols. 2 and 3 by Ian Colvin), 3 vols. (London: Victor Gollancz, 1932–36).

6. On the issue of devolution in Scotland and Wales see Great Britain, Privy Council, *Devolution within the United Kingdom: Some Alternatives for Discussion* (London: HMSO, 1974), and *Our Changing Democracy: Devolution to Scotland and Wales*, Cmnd. 6348 (London: HMSO, 1975); Vernon Bogdanor, *Devolution* (London: Oxford University Press, 1979); and H. M. Drucker and Gordon Brown, *The Politics of Nationalism and Devolution* (London: Longman, 1980).

7. On the distinctive character of Ulster politics see Richard Rose, *Governing without Consensus* (Boston: Beacon Press, 1971); and Liam de Paor, *Divided Ulster* (Harmondsworth: Penguin, 1970).

the divisions between the majority and minority communities.

Nevertheless, it is highly probable that if Prior patiently persists with his scheme none of the major parties in Ulster will wish to risk abstaining from the elections. And once the assembly is in being, the hope would be that political cooperation and creative political thinking cutting across sectarian and party lines will reemerge and create its own momentum. Certainly there is a far graver risk if the vacuum in the political life of the province is left to be exploited by the paramilitaries and the bigoted extremists.

Even if Prior's projects for political reform and economic and social regeneration do bear fruit, we should be under no illusions that they will be the panacea for ending what has become the most intractable terrorist conflict in Western European experience. For, indeed, the closer Prior and the moderate politicians in Northern Ireland come to establishing a stable and legitimate government acceptable to a majority of both majority and minority communities, the more frenetically the extremists on both sides will try to undermine and destroy it by terrorism, street violence, and possibly by disruptive industrial action.

The possibility that efforts at political progress may stimulate further violence is not a reason for abandoning the effort at democratic political innovation and constructive reform. But the British government and public should realize that no system of assembly government, however skillfully designed and devotedly executed, is a panacea for ending the terrorism. On the contrary, success in the battle to curb terrorism is a precondition for the long-term viability of any democratic government involving the participation of both majority and minority communities.

And if we are to fully understand the complexity and intractability of the conflict, we must remember that the province is plagued by two warring traditions of extremism and violence, Loyalist and Republican. All those who resort to terrorism in a democratic society, brutally blotting out the rights of their fellow citizens, are equally reprehensible and should be unequivocally condemned. The men of violence on both sides of the sectarian divide must be deterred or subdued if democratic politics and reconciliation in Northern Ireland are to have a chance. In resolving this problem of order, the British government therefore deserves the fullest support of the Opposition at Westminster and of our democratic allies in Ireland and America, for their moral and political support and cooperation in security matters are vital to the defeat of terrorism in the North.

Orange Extremism

The Ulster Defence Association, the Ulster Volunteer Force, the Red Hand Commandos, and the Ulster Freedom Fighters have committed hundreds of crimes, including many brutal sectarian murders, bombings, and arson attacks on Catholic homes, pubs, clubs, hotels, and other targets.[8] They have frequently aimed at creating mass slaughter. Though the vast majority of these attacks have been mounted in Northern Ireland, they have occasionally struck at targets in the Republic. For example, on Friday, May 17, 1974, Protestant terrorists set off four large car bombs in the Republic—three in Dublin and one in the border town of Monaghan—killing twenty-eight people. They have committed particularly brutal campaigns of sectarian murder in the North. In some phases of the conflict five Catholics were murdered for every two Protestants. One Catholic victim was lured from a pub, cruelly beaten, strangled, and his body suspended from iron railings. The IRA has no monopoly of brutality.

Orange extremism, bigotry, and intimidation bear a heavy responsibility for provoking open conflict in the late 1960s and for creating the conditions in which the Provisional IRA could be created and grow in the Catholic ghettos.[9] The two traditions of extremism feed on each other. If the Reverend Ian

8. For a detailed account see Martin Dillon and Denis Lehane, *Political Murder in Northern Ireland* (Harmondsworth: Penguin, 1973).
9. London *Sunday Times* Insight Team, *Ulster* (Harmondsworth: Penguin, 1972).

Paisley did not exist as the physical embodiment of Protestant bigotry and sectarian hatred, the IRA would need to create him.

The present-day manifestations of Orange extremism are the Reverend Ian Paisley's Democratic Union party (DUP) and the paramilitary organizations such as the Ulster Defence Association (UDA), the Orange Volunteers, and the so-called Third Force set up by Paisley in 1981. At the terrorist end of the spectrum are the Red Hand Commandos, the Ulster Freedom Fighters (UFF), and the Ulster Volunteer Force (UVF), which is named after Carson's private army of the pre–World War I period.

The Orange extremists are just as much prisoners of the past as the IRA, and, like Republican extremists, they are much given to romanticizing and glorifying the use of violence to attain political goals. Every Protestant child is reminded of the victories of William of Orange over the Catholic army of James II in the Civil War of 1688–91. The Orangemen to this day celebrate King Billy's victory in the Battle of the Boyne (1960) and the relief of Londonderry (1689).

It is superficial to see the gulf between the Protestants and Catholics of Northern Ireland in purely sectarian terms: it is truly an ethnic divide.[10] The first major settlement of Protestants in the North occurred in the early years of the seventeenth century when King James I made a grant of land to Scottish Presbyterians to settle in Ulster. But unlike those settlers who, in the same period, went to colonize North America, the Protestant plantations in Ulster were not founded in a wilderness inhabited by red Indians. They took the land from the native Catholic population and sought to impose their religion upon them. No wonder they reaped a bitter harvest.

The Ulster Protestants have always seen themselves as Britons, loyal to the Protestant crown. The Catholics, on the other hand, have always regarded themselves as primarily Irish, sharing the same culture and traditions as their coreligionists in the

10. This divide has been explored by Conor Cruise O'Brien in his classic study *States of Ireland* (London: Panther, 1974).

rest of Ireland. These differences have been sustained and deepened by the segregation of schooling and cultural and political life on sectarian lines and by three centuries of conflict.

At the beginning of this century Ulster Protestants watched with alarm as successive Liberal governments at Westminster sought to introduce home rule into Ireland. They saw this as a threat to their Protestant ascendancy and way of life. Between 1906 and 1915, under the powerful leadership of Sir Edward Carson, a Protestant private army of eighty thousand volunteers (the UVF) was organized to resist any attempt by the Asquith government to impose home rule on Ulster.

The partition imposed by the Anglo-Irish Treaty of 1921 recognized the intransigent demand of Protestant Ulster to remain united with the United Kingdom. The six northern counties that formed the territory of the new state under the Stormont government found themselves in the vicelike grip of the Protestant Unionism. IRA attempts to mobilize armed rebellion against the Stormont government in 1938–39 and 1956–62 were swiftly suppressed.

Yet even when the Unionist ascendancy seemed most secure and the Westminster government almost invincibly ignorant and apathetic about the internal affairs of the province, Orange extremism continued to thrive mightily. The marches and drumbeats of the Orange Order and the Apprentice Boys, the public displays of Ulster Unionist identity and pride, were matters of religious observance. Any efforts, however modest, to redress Catholic grievances concerning discrimination in jobs and housing were flatly rejected. And even the most routine political contacts with the government of the Republic were seen as treason by the self-appointed guardians of Ulster Protestantism. They still are to this day.

The truth is that the Ulster Protestants have the mentality of a beleaguered minority. They have never shaken off the fear that someday the overwhelmingly Catholic Republic of Ireland will try to absorb or annex them. Far from being reassured by direct rule from Westminster, since the abolition of the Stormont government in 1972, their sense of insecurity has been increased because they feel they no longer have direct political control over their affairs. They are haunted by the idea of a "sellout," and the 1980 and 1981 "summits" between the prime ministers of Ireland and the United Kingdom and the 1981 agreement to establish an intergovernmental Anglo-Irish Council for cooperation on trade and security have deepened their suspicion. Paisley and other Protestant extremists have been quick to exploit this fear.

There are, of course, perfectly understandable reasons why the overwhelming majority of Protestants fear unification with the Republic. In Northern Ireland the one-million-strong Protestant population can ensure that their religious and political rights and way of life are fully protected. There are only half a million Catholics in Northern Ireland, and the Protestants do not believe that demographic trends will threaten Unionist dominance for the foreseeable future. If they were to be united with the Republic, however, the thirty-two counties would comprise 1.2 million Protestants and 3.3 million Catholics. The Protestants' major fears are that in a reunited Ireland they would lose their previous link with the British crown and be forced to give up their religious and civil rights. For example, they would lose the legal rights to divorce, abortion, and contraception. And they fear that their children would be submitted to a Catholic-dominated Irish education system.[11]

These are reasonable and tangible concerns, as the last Irish prime minister, Garret Fitzgerald, recognized when he bravely embarked on his "constitutional crusade" to amend the Republic's Constitution to allay the fears of the Ulster Protestants. He also repeatedly reassured Ulstermen that his government would not seek to coerce Ulster into unification and has even proposed amending the Irish Constitution to rescind all claims to sovereignty over the territory of Northern Ireland.

Though moderate Protestants in the North may be slightly

11. For discussion of the effects of sectarian division on children and the education system see, for example, Morris Fraser, *Children in Conflict* (New York: Basic Books, 1977); and James L. Russell, *Civic Education in Northern Ireland* (Belfast: Northern Ireland Community Relations Commission, 1972).

reassured by Dr. Fitzgerald's statesmanlike moderation and sensitivity, the new prime minister, Charles Haughey, is regarded with grave suspicion because of his alleged role in gun-running for the IRA in the early 1970s. The Orange extremists see a conspiracy to "sell out" Ulster behind every bush. They are now busily denouncing an alleged "deal" or "conspiracy" between the Dublin and Westminster governments and are thereby making the task of the British government, patiently seeking to mediate between the two communities and attempting to find a stable form of government for the province acceptable to the moderates of both sides, immeasurably more difficult. Bizarre recent manifestations of extreme Unionist paranoia are the allegations by Enoch Powell of a longstanding conspiracy between the British Foreign Office and the U.S. government to sell out Ulster and to take the newly unified Ireland into NATO, and by James Molyneaux that the CIA is implicated in terrorist murders in Ulster. Only in the strange world of Ulster politics could two leading political figures survive in public life after making such serious charges while failing to provide a scrap of evidence to support them.

The leading personality of the Orange extremists is the Reverend Ian Paisley, a big man with a powerful voice and a talent for inflammatory speeches. His hatred of Catholicism is so vitriolic that his attacks on the pope seem like a throwback to the Reformation. Paisley sees Catholicism as an unmitigated evil and the pope as antichrist. Amazingly, he fills his church every Sunday, has successfully founded his own Free Presbyterian church, his own Democratic Unionist party, and his own paramilitary Third Force. In June 1979 he was elected as one of three European Parliament members for Northern Ireland with a total of 170,688 votes.[12]

Ironically, Paisley and his followers played a major part in creating the last twelve years of conflict, a crisis he has been successful in exploiting. It was Paisley who played on the fears of Orangemen in the late 1960s, portraying the demonstrations

12. See "After the European Elections," *Government and Opposition* 14 (Autumn 1979): 411–507.

of the Northern Ireland Civil Rights Association (NICRA) as a preliminary to armed rebellion. It was Paisley who helped cause the collapse of the Ulster police system in 1969–70 by bringing Protestant toughs out on the streets to intimidate and harass the Catholic protesters, provoking a backlash from the Republican ghettos and creating a situation the Royal Ulster Constabulary and the "B Specials" could no longer control.[13]

Nor should we forget that it was Paisley's movement, using intimidation, that enabled the Ulster Workers' Council strike of 1974 to paralyze the public utilities and thus to undermine the power-sharing Northern Ireland Executive. This pioneering power-sharing with its democratic assembly, and an Executive led by Brian Faulkner (a moderate Unionist) and Gerry Fitt of the Catholic Social Democratic and Labour Party (SDLP), was the brightest hope for long-term peace and stability in the decade. Paisley was not alone in opposing it, but there is no doubt that his dedicated opposition was one of the key factors in its destruction. The secret of Paisley's success is his skill as an opportunist and populist politician, playing on the fears of the Protestant population and projecting an image of himself as the only man capable of uncompromising and full-blooded defense of the rights of Protestant Ulster. In a sense his mass political movement, the DUP, is both cause and consequence of the polarization of Ulster politics in the period of the terrorist emergency. He has been able to weaken the middle ground of politics by portraying the moderate Unionists as fudgers and appeasers who cannot be relied upon to defend Ulster's rights. At the same time he has encouraged paramilitarism and direct action by the Orange extremists, and, as demonstrated twice in his use of the general strike as a weapon against the authorities in Northern Ireland, he and his followers well understand the utility of intimidation as a weapon to coerce the Protestant community if peaceful persuasion fails.

In its propaganda the Provisional IRA points to Paisleyite bigotry and intransigence as further evidence of the justice of "the

13. Richard Clutterbuck, *Guerrillas and Terrorists* (London: Faber and Faber, 1977), pp. 65–66.

cause." Paisley, for his part, constantly preys on Protestant fears of PIRA terrorism and presents his own policy as the only one capable of beating the Provisionals into the ground. Thus Orange and Green extremism constitute a mutually feeding process, frequently flaring up into campaigns of tit-for-tat sectarian murder and creating more sectarian fear, hatred, and suspicion, which inevitably undermine the middle ground of political compromise and dialogue between the majority and minority communities.

Unfortunately, the moderate Official Unionist party was badly split by disagreements over the 1973–74 initiative and has never fully recovered. It has also lacked a leader of sufficient charisma and political flair to act as an effective counterweight to Paisley's noisy populism and to serve as a rallying point for moderate Protestants.

There are grave dangers in the Reverend Paisley's power game. He is probably waiting for an opportunity to declare, and claim the leadership of, an independent Ulster regime. He almost certainly does not understand the economic impact of a total break with Britain. He would probably expect to be the leader of the new Orange microstate. Who can doubt that the rights of the Catholic minority in a Paisleyite state would go to the wall? Paisley would probably try to use his paramilitary Third Force to suppress all resistance from the Catholic population and to destroy any other dissident group. Already Paisley's creation of the Third Force has provoked Republican extremists to retaliate by creating a Fourth Force, and Paisley's threatening speeches, and the marching feet of his private army, are only helping the IRA to increase recruitment and to find more excuses for violence.

Most damaging of all, Paisley is implicitly challenging the security forces and raising the threat of civil war on two fronts against the constitutional authorities. Further dangers lie in Paisley's attempts to split the Royal Ulster Constabulary and other key organs of administration in Northern Ireland.

It is heartening to see that many moderate Unionists have come out firmly in opposition to Paisley. One Unionist spokesman, Robert McCartney, Q.C., has had the courage to challenge Paisley on a public platform, warning his countrymen of what he sees as the sinister antidemocratic implications of Paisley's recent actions.

The Provisional IRA

The history of Irish Republicanism, and of the Irish Republican Army in particular, has been brilliantly described in Conor Cruise O'Brien's essay. I will instead briefly sketch the characteristics of the Provisional IRA organization of today.[14] The Provisional IRA is an offspring of the original Irish Republican Army, which fought against the British in the war of Irish independence, 1919–21. The IRA leaders accused Michael Collins and the other Irish leaders who supported the Anglo-Irish Treaty of betrayal because the terms of the treaty left Ireland divided into a Protestant Unionist state in the North and the independent Irish Free State in the South.

The Ulster Unionists led by Edward Carson threatened to resist any effort to integrate them with the predominantly Catholic Free State, and the Lloyd George government, having no stomach for a further civil war in Ireland, gave way to the pressure for partition. In the Dail (parliament) in Dublin the treaty was adopted after a bitter debate by sixty-four votes to fifty-seven. There followed a bloody civil war in which the IRA fought the Free State forces, killed more Irishmen in the South than in the North, and assassinated Michael Collins in 1922.

Even though the IRA was defeated in the civil war by 1923, the movement's hard-core militants never gave up their aim of uniting Ireland by force. They developed the classic features of a secret terrorist organization and launched bombing and murder campaigns in the North in the late 1930s and again in 1956–62. By the early 1960s, when it became clear that the armed struggle was failing to attract Catholic support in the

14. For a fuller assessment see Paul Wilkinson, "The Provisional IRA: An Assessment in the Wake of the 1981 Hunger Strike," *Government and Opposition* 17 (Spring 1982): 140–56.

North, the official IRA leadership was taken over by Marxists and intellectuals who changed the priorities of the movement. Their main aim became the ending of what they saw as a capitalist regime in Dublin, and the assimilation of the North into a united Ireland took on a more incidental role dependent upon appropriate economic conditions.

In the mid and late 1960s, when politics in the North were becoming more sharply polarized on sectarian lines, the Northern Ireland Civil Rights Association was making the running, demanding reforms to end discrimination against the one-half million Catholic minority population in Ulster. Paisley and militant Protestants reacted violently against the NICRA campaign. Serious rioting occurred in 1969 in Belfast and Londonderry, and it soon became clear that the Royal Ulster Constabulary was incapable of guaranteeing the rights of peaceful demonstrations and protest. Catholic community leaders believed that the "B Specials" deliberately allowed Protestant youths to attack Catholic citizens and their property. After the serious riots in Londonderry in August 1969, the Labour home secretary, James Callaghan, decided that the Ulster police system had broken down and committed the army in support of the civil power to restore order, initially with the purpose of protecting the Catholic population.[15]

By 1970 militant Catholics had turned against the British army and were angry and resentful that the official IRA had done nothing to defend them against Protestant attacks. IRA "I Ran Away" graffiti appeared on the walls of the Catholic ghettos. And in 1970 a new organization, the Provisional IRA ("Provisional" in memory of the provisional government declared by the leaders of the Easter Rising in Dublin 1916), was formed with the self-appointed tasks of defending the Catholic community and throwing out the British army and the police. It rapidly established a secret army of "brigades" and "battalions" based on the Catholic parish districts and accumulated young

15. See the Rt. Hon. James Callaghan's personal account in *A House Divided* (London: Collins, 1972).

recruits from working-class Republican areas, stores of rifles, explosives, and other weapons. It developed into a ruthless terrorist organization mounting bombing and shooting attacks on police, soldiers, commercial premises, and civilians, with increasing indiscriminateness and ferocity. For example, the IRA bombed the Le Mon House Hotel when there were seven hundred people, including women and children, inside, and it has attacked the Royal Victoria Hospital, Belfast, and shopping centers in Northern Ireland, London, and other mainland cities. On November 21, 1974 it bombed pubs in Birmingham, killing 19 and injuring 202. It has tarred and feathered, kneecapped, and murdered its own people as "punishment" for informing or other alleged crimes. It has even booby-trapped the bodies of murdered British soldiers so as to explode at touch. The Provisionals continued their terrorist campaign with the same fanaticism even after the Stormont system of Unionist-dominated government in the province had been dismantled, direct rule from Westminster had been introduced, and all the major Catholic grievances concerning discrimination had been remedied by legislation.

The Provisionals' overriding aim is to sicken the British government and public of the task of governing Northern Ireland to the point of withdrawal. To the twenty-two million Americans of Irish descent whom they look to for funds and arms they like to present themselves as freedom fighters against British colonial repression. In reality they have other aims which they do not wish to be publicized in the United States. A leading Provisional spokesman stated in a November 1978 interview with the Italian Red Brigades' organ, *Contro Informazione*: "We must educate the workers to destabilize capitalism in the whole of Ireland through armed struggle, creating an irremediable conflict between the needs of local capitalism and international imperialism, and those of the popular masses."[16] And Rory O'Brady, president of Provisional Sinn Fein (the political party wing of the Provisionals) and leading political

16. *Contro Informazione*, November 1978.

strategist of the movement, admitted in another newspaper interview the desire to create a "Democratic Socialist Republic . . . similar to communism but not exactly like it"[17] as a one-party dictatorship for the whole of Ireland. Thus the Provisional IRA is a direct threat to the survival of parliamentary democracy south as well as north of the border.

It is estimated the PIRA has three hundred or so terrorist operatives (gunmen, bombers, commanders, and others) and about two thousand supporters (who provide propaganda support, collect funds, and provide safe houses). Overall direction comes from the Dublin headquarters, where the most influential personalities are Sinn Fein president, Rory O'Brady, and vice-president, David O'Connell. The leadership in the North is based in Belfast and often has strong differences of opinion with the Dublin leadership: in Belfast Gerry Adams and Ivor Bell are among the main strategists.

In 1977 the PIRA discarded its traditional "army" structure of "brigades" and "battalions" and adopted the tight-knit cellular structure characteristic of Continental terrorist groups. Only the leader of each cell has links to the directorate and other cells. This structure makes the PIRA terrorist groups a more difficult quarry for the police, but the price that they have paid for clandestinity is greater isolation from the grass-roots politics of the Catholic community in the North.

The Provisionals' press and propaganda campaign, operating from its press center in Belfast and led by experienced and skilled propagandists such as Danny Morrison, Richard McAuley and Joe Austen is a crucial part of the IRA effort. This team successfully exploited the Maze hunger strike, particularly in the American and other international media. They whipped up emotive support for Noraid and other Provisional support groups in the United States, and undoubtedly many of those who gave funds to these groups did not realize their money would provide weapons for a continuing murder campaign in Northern Ireland and not simply support the families of IRA

17. In an interview with *Il Giornale Nuovo* (Milan), September 2, 1979.

prisoners. The harsh reality is that these PIRA support groups collected an estimated $250,000 in the first six months of 1981. The bulk of PIRA weaponry now comes from U.S. sources, and the FBI has recently uncovered a direct arms supply route via Noraid to the PIRA.

The PIRA has also obtained millions of pounds over recent years from protection rackets, armed robbery, drug smuggling, and other criminal activities, north and south of the border. In 1978–79 it got £5 million from bank robberies in the Republic alone. And in 1979 four IRA men were caught with $2.3 million worth of marijuana hidden in a truckload of bananas.[18]

The PIRA also values highly its links with foreign terrorist movements such as the Popular Front for the Liberation of Palestine, the Red Brigades, the Red Army Faction, and the ETA. For example, an Italian Red Brigade member revealed in 1980 that Italian terrorists had shared a huge consignment of Palestinian weapons between the ETA and the IRA. In November 1977 the S.S. *Towerstream* was seized off Antwerp with half a million dollars worth of weapons destined for the PIRA and routed from Lebanon via Cyprus. Colonel Qadaffi of Libya has also provided generous supplies of Soviet-made arms and propaganda support. In an interview the Libyan leader declared that "aid to PIRA enables us to kill 3 birds with one stone . . . ; we pay Great Britain back in some way, even though minimally, for the harm she has done and continues to do to our countries."[19]

The PIRA used the 1981 Maze hunger strike to reap emotive propaganda, to restore the flow of cash and weapons from the previously dwindling U.S. sources, and to regroup and rearm. But it also incurred grave liabilities. The Catholic church leaders and politicians in the Republic became sickened by the callous inhumanity of an organization that was sentencing its own members to commit suicide in prison as a method of

18. *International Herald Tribune*, August 28, 1979.
19. Quoted in Claire Sterling, *The Terror Network: The Secret War of International Terrorism* (New York: Reader's Digest Press/Holt, Rinehart, and Winston, 1981).

blackmail. Pressure from priests and the prisoners' families eventually broke the hunger strike. And at the end of the day the British government had the courage to stand firm and refused to concede what the PIRA really wanted: "political status," special privileges for convicted criminals merely on the ground that they were members of the PIRA. No democratic government worthy of the name could have conceded such a demand.

Nevertheless, by its recent outrages the PIRA has shown that it is still in the business of murder. Along with Paisley and his bigoted paramilitary supporters, the PIRA constitutes the major obstacle to the development of peace and reconciliation in Northern Ireland. If the lives of the innocent are to be protected and if law and democracy are to be upheld, terrorism must be subdued.

Are there any general lessons to be drawn by liberal democratic governments from the history of the Northern Ireland conflict? Successive British governments, the Royal Ulster Constabulary, and the British army have all undoubtedly gained a knowledge of the problems of responding to terrorism in a liberal democracy which is probably unrivaled among the Western allies.[20]

The British army was called in as a last resort for peacekeeping duties in Northern Ireland in 1970 because the civil police system had broken down under the impact of sectarian manipulation and civil violence. But no British government has ever tried to adopt a strategy of totally militarizing the response to terrorism, of suspending the judicial process, or of abandoning civil administration and democratic politics in Northern Ireland. These extreme measures have been resorted to in many other countries, but in Northern Ireland, even though the province has experienced the most protracted and intensive terrorist campaign in Western Europe since 1945, the British

20. For discussions of the army and police responses see Paul Wilkinson, ed., *British Perspectives on Terrorism* (London: George Allen and Unwin, 1981).

authorities have been determined to maintain democratic rights and government and to combat terrorism by the traditional democratic means of judicial control, albeit strengthened in certain respects by emergency provisions.[21]

The outward and visible signs of the success of the judicial control response have been the reshouldering, since 1976, of the major burden of combating terrorist crime by the civil police, the Royal Ulster Constabulary, reformed and modernized on nonsectarian lines; a concomitant reduction in the role of the British army, now mainly confined to countering terrorism in the border areas too dangerous for normal policing; the gradual reduction in the number of deaths from terrorism from 467 in 1972 to 75 in 1980; and the increasing number of convictions for serious crimes committed by Republican and Loyalist terrorists secured in the courts and the greater flow of trust, information, and cooperation from the public to the police which makes these successes possible.

The Northern Ireland conflict has also shown very clearly the severe limitations of terrorism as a weapon. Terrorist atrocities have secured plenty of publicity for the terrorists and their various threats and demands, but these propaganda "victories" should not delude anyone into thinking that terrorists of either extreme have "won" their wars. On the contrary, terrorism has only tended to stiffen the determination and intransigence of the adversary community. Violence and sectarian attacks by one set of extremists inevitably provoke counterterror and defensive paramilitarism from the other.

The Northern Ireland conflict is exceptional in Western Europe because it is a classic case of ethnic minority terrorism: the Provisional IRA, a tiny minority of the Catholic minority population in Northern Ireland, seeks to "liberate" a territory in which the majority refuse to be liberated. Meanwhile, the Orange extremists, fearful of being made a disadvantaged minority in a Catholic Irish Republic, are ready to wage a bloody civil war if necessary to prevent any attempt at unification.

21. For example, the Northern Ireland (Emergency Provisions) Act, 1973, and the Prevention of Terrorism (Temporary Provisions) Act, 1974.

There is thus no simple political solution to this problem that would, at a stroke, remove the underlying causes of the terrorism. All one can dare to hope for is a gradual healing of some of the wounds of sectarian conflict and hatred and, in the longer term, a slow movement toward reconciliation and cooperation between the Catholic and Protestant communities. Tragically, the terrorism that is produced by the hatred and fanaticism of the conflict has created its own momentum: hatred and fear breed terrorism, which in turn creates more hatred and fear. No British government can, by itself, succeed in breaking this cycle of terror. The will for peace and reconciliation must come from the people of Northern Ireland in both communities. And the governments and publics of both the United Kingdom and the Republic of Ireland will need to show fortitude and courage in working together to combat terrorism, to improve cross-border antiterrorist cooperation, and to encourage the moderate democratic parties of both communities in the North to work for a more stable and peaceful future together.

7

Total Terrorism: Argentina, 1969 to 1979

An Extreme Case

Throughout the 1970s, Argentina was a laboratory for terrorism. In the first half of the decade terrorism became an integral part of everyday life and seemed likely to become endemic, like gangsterism in Chicago in the 1920s. But by the end of 1979 official barbarism had surpassed that of the terrorists in savagery. Argentina, rich in anomalies and long held up to the world as an extravagantly bad example of almost everything, from its telephone system to its catastrophic rate of inflation, became a terrorist state without terrorists.

My aim in this essay is to describe how this came about. I have tried to put together a human document, drawing on my own experience and primary sources (which I have not footnoted, for security reasons) for the benefit of other scholars. I hope that this treatment may throw up some ideas for research which might not emerge in more scholarly treatises.

Argentina is, of course, an extreme case of a society besieged by terrorism. The forms of terrorism that developed in Argentina over more than a decade, under constantly changing conditions, were so many and so varied that they provide the researcher with a wide choice of case studies.

In the early 1960s, two attempts to establish guerrilla "focos" in northern Argentina failed. These were Cuban-inspired adventures. But even Ernesto (Che) Guevara himself did not think that a successful guerrilla war could be fought in his native land at a time when the military were returning the country to limited democracy. (Peronists, who made up the majority party, were not allowed to put up their own candidates in the 1963 elections.) In an apocryphal story that captures the drift of Guevara's philosophy, he is supposed to have remarked that nobody could conduct a successful guerrilla war against a government headed by an amiable country doctor. Dr. Arturo Illia, a middle-of-the-road Radical, had been elected president with less than a quarter of the votes cast. He fell to a military coup, but under his government the armed forces suppressed incipient guerrilla movements with ease. A putative terrorist movement in Buenos Aires also self-aborted when a bomb factory in a residential hotel apartment blew up.

The tapestry woven by terrorism in Argentina is complex, intricate, and ever-changing in pattern. Terrorism failed abysmally when confronted by the unrepresentative, highly inefficient, but basically decent government of Illia. It became hyperactive during the dying years of the military dictatorship that had ousted Illia in 1966. The virulence of terrorist violence accelerated the military's retreat from government. Yet when a truly representative government took office under Hector Campora (elected with almost 50 percent of the votes in March 1973) and Juan Domingo Peron himself (who won an unprecedented 62.8 percent of the poll in September 1974), the terrorists went from strength to strength. By the beginning of 1975 they believed that power was within their grasp.

I believe that the terrorists' successes are attributable to many factors—psychological, social, and political, some peculiarly Argentine, others applicable anywhere—but that they were also aided by the cupidity and stupidity of members of the

Peronist "royal family" and the internal dissension within the ruling Peronist coalition. Peron was too old and too ill to hold the disintegrating Peronist movement together. His death in mid-1974 left his unpopular widow, "Isabelita," in power. Behind her throne was a contemporary Rasputin, José Lopez Rega, a man who believed he had mystical powers and claimed that he took dictation from the archangel Gabriel. He met Isabelita through a shared interest in spiritualism. A retired police corporal, he became her secretary and, eventually, the controller of the Peron household. When Peron took over the presidency he made Lopez Rega, by then his private secretary, minister of social welfare, a position of great power and influence.

The Black Night Begins

Within two years, Lopez Rega had earned himself a niche in Argentine history as an archetypal scoundrel. Parents hissed his name to frighten their children into good behavior. He also served as a useful scapegoat for everything that went wrong in Argentina. Lopez Rega was depicted as the evil genius behind the right-wing death squads that had begun to overwhelm the left-wing killers and outnumbered them by five to one in the quantity of corpses they left strewn along the highways and byways of Argentina. He was blamed for the economic crisis which Peron left as his legacy. Finally, he fell foul of the military.

To save him from an end as sinister as his own background, Isabelita sent him to Europe as her "ambassador-at-large to the Old World" [sic] in July 1975. Once in Europe, he disappeared like a fugitive. Significantly, the Argentine government has never bothered to go through the motions of tracing him. There have been a few half-hearted efforts by judges, investigating corruption charges brought against Mrs. Peron and her coterie, to secure his return to Argentina to stand trial for fraud and embezzlement of public funds but, to no one's surprise, various sightings of him that have been reported in the press have never been followed up.

Within a year of the departure of her Svengali, Mrs. Peron had been overthrown. On March 24, 1976, the entire Argentine nation heaved an audible sigh of relief when it awoke to discover that—as it was reported then—a bloodless coup had taken place overnight. Argentina's nightmare seemed to be over. In fact, Argentina's black night of total terrorism had just begun. By the end of the year, left-wing terrorism and right-wing terrorism had claimed close to one thousand known victims. What was not known—and is still a secret today—was the full toll of the total terrorism, which, behind a curtain of self-censorship, was gnawing at the nation's entrails. The fallout of fear from the methods being used to counter terrorism proved to be almost 100 percent effective. It was probably unnecessary to make as many as fifty-nine journalists "disappear" (which is the documented number of members of the press who have vanished after being abducted, presumably by members of the security forces) or kill another forty.[1] The media soon got the message not to report what the military government did not want reported, although, for the benefit of the handful of newspapers that tried to keep their readers vaguely informed of what was going on, the ban on the reporting of the appearance of cadavers, of kidnappings, and disappearances (the word was quickly accepted into the vocabulary with its new meaning) was put on the record in an unsigned order.[2]

The word *desaparecido* was not unknown before the coup. There had been two notorious cases of disappearances—a couple called Verd in Mendoza and a lawyer and his client, who were kidnapped on a Buenos Aires street and never heard of again. When human rights organizations began to monitor the disappearances a few months after the coup, they discovered that clandestine detentions had begun in earnest in the four months before the coup.

1. Two sources of information about the pressure on the press in Argentina, by terrorists of the right, of the left, and of the state, are Andrew Graham-Yooll, *The Press in Argentina 1973–8* (London: Writers and Scholars Educational Trust, 1979); and Robert Cox, *The Sound of One Hand Clapping: A Preliminary Study of the Argentine Press in a Time of Terror* (Washington, D.C.: The Wilson Center, 1980).
2. See Cox, *The Sound of One Hand Clapping*, p. 9.

In Spanish the word *desaparecido* is sometimes used as a tasteful euphemism to indicate that someone has died. That is almost the precise meaning of "disappeared" today, except that it means that the disappeared person has probably been killed by the security forces in one of at least ten secret detention camps[3] set up by the armed forces commanders after the coup. The number of people who have disappeared in Argentina since 1975 is still unknown. The minimum figure is some six thousand.[4] But many human rights workers believe that for every case reported to them, there are at least three other missing people, whose families are frightened to approach the often harassed and constantly threatened organizations that try to record human rights violations in Argentina. My own estimate is that at least ten to twelve thousand people have disappeared after being abducted by the security forces. That figure is also based on contact with families who have not reported the disappearance of their relatives for a variety of reasons. (Some parents have actually been told by high-ranking officers that their children are being held in clandestine prisons and that they will be released one day if their relatives maintain a prudent silence and are patient.) In several cases, children have been allowed to telephone their parents from their secret places of detention. All have urged their parents not to take legal action.[5]

The Argentine Dream

Argentines, despite a bloody early history, do not consider themselves a violent people. A popular joke, which remained

3. See Amnesty International, *The Disappeared of Argentina and Testimony on Secret Detention Camps in Argentina* (London: Amnesty International, 1979).

4. See Inter-American Commission on Human Rights, *Report on the Situation of Human Rights in Argentina* (Washington, D.C.: Organization of American States, 1980), p. 148; and Amnesty International publications on Argentina. The best source for information on disappearances and human rights violations in Argentina is the Centro de Estudios Legales y Sociales, Sarmiento 1562, 5 to "C," 1042-Buenos Aires, Argentina.

5. Correspondence in the possession of the author, some of which can be made available, confidentially.

current up until 1973, claimed that more people were hurt at a Mexican wedding than in an Argentine coup d'etat. It is impossible for many Argentines to believe today that terrorism could summon up such horrors from the deep of the Argentine psyche.

Given the picture that Argentines have of themselves, a vision encapsulating all the wishful thinking of these twenty-six million transplanted Europeans who still half believe that they are perfecting the old civilization of their ancestors in more benevolent climes, their ostrichlike behavior when faced with the terrible troubles and traumas that terrorism brings in its wake is perfectly understandable. Haunted, as most Argentines are, by the belief that Western civilization will destroy itself one day, leaving them as the sole survivors capable of carrying on its traditions and culture, it was hard enough for them to believe that Argentine society could come close to disintegration under the assault of escalating terrorism. It was, and still is, impossible for civilized Argentines to believe that the security forces could become even more barbaric than the terrorists. Argentines believe they are the heirs to Western, Christian civilization. No reality is strong enough to disturb that dream. Indeed, when reality is so unpleasant and appears to deny the dream it becomes even more compelling to escape into the fantasy land of the mind.

Any suggestion that Argentina is not as Argentines believe it to be is dismissed as "anti-Argentine propaganda." The dream country that Argentines have chosen to inhabit is so perfect that it is not surprising that they are convinced that the rest of the world is enviously conspiring against them.[6]

The Violent Argentine Reality

From June 30, 1969, when Augusto Vandor, the most outstanding leader produced by the Argentine labor movement, was

6. Some insight into Argentine self-perceptions is offered in Jacobo Timerman, *Prisoner without a Name, Cell without a Number* (New York: Alfred A. Knopf, 1981); V. S. Naipul, *The Return of Evita Peron* (London: Andrew

assassinated (this murder is the first officially attributed to terrorists by the military government) terrorism spread like wildfire. The following statistics are taken from the most recent of the government's own reports on terrorism.[7] The figures are not particularly accurate (to make a better case for the government in defending it against charges that it condoned violations of human rights, the compilers included a number of murders carried out by the security forces themselves). The total number of incidents each year also seems to be an arbitrary figure, meant to demonstrate the return of law and order to the country after the military takeover rather than to give an accurate picture of terrorist activities. Nevertheless, the annual totals fairly reflect the expansion of terrorism after the elected Peronist coalition government took office in May 1973, and they also demonstrate that terrorism was out of control when the armed forces took over in 1976.[8]

1969: One murder, two kidnappings, and an attempted abduction.

1970: Four murders, three kidnappings, and two short-lived takeovers of two very small townships.

1971: 26 murders out of a total of 35 terrorist incidents.

1972: 25 murders out of 35 terrorist incidents.

Deutsch, 1980), also available in a U.S. edition; and James Neilson, *La voragine argentina* (Buenos Aires: Marymar, 1979).

7. *Observations and Criticisms Made by the Government of Argentina with Regard to the Report of the Inter-American Commission on Human Rights on the Situation of Human Rights in Argentina* (Washington, D.C.: Organization of American States, 1980).

8. For comparison of statistics see also *El terrorismo en la Argentina* (Argentine government publication produced by the Ministry of Interior, September 1979) and *Argentina y sus derechos humanos* (Buenos Aires, 1978), a publication attributed to the Asociacion Patriotica Argentina, an organization I was never able to run to earth despite repeated efforts. The book, which is largely composed of horrendous photographs of mutilated corpses, including atrocities committed by right-wing parapolice organizations but attributed to the left, could not have been compiled without access to police files. It was initially distributed by the Ministry of Interior. But official endorsement of this incredibly crude and unwittingly self-accusatory work was withdrawn when members of the government became aware of its negative impact on members of the diplomatic corps and foreign press. Needless to say, it is totally unreliable as a record of terrorist crimes, but it does provide a revealing insight into the mentality of the security forces.

1973: 58 murders out of a total of 136 terrorist crimes.
1974: 110 murdered during 187 attacks.
1975: 346 killed during a total of 194 terrorist attacks.
1976: 646 murders in 298 attacks. (The military took over on March 24.)
1977: 181 killed in 82 incidents.
1978: 100 killings in only 36 recorded incidents.
1979: Terrorist killings down to seven among only six recorded terrorist strikes.

Throughout 1980 and 1981 there was virtually no left-wing terrorist activity within Argentina. There were also very few recorded instances of disappearances. It seems reasonable to assume that a decision was made not to continue with the tactic of making people "disappear" and that this was enforced. The climate of fear within Argentina remained so intense, however, that it is possible that a few people are still disappearing but that their families and friends are under such extreme intimidation that they are afraid to report these cases. Two cases of disappearances alleged to have taken place in 1981 were reported by the Centro de Estudios Legales y Sociales (see note 4) in January 1982. Although one of these cases was fraudulent—a young man, Daniel Alejandro Di Bernardo, simulated his own disappearance in an attempt to secure a visa to reside in Sweden—human rights workers believe that there may be other disappearances that have not been reported because of threats of reprisals.[9]

9. It is significant that although the Federal Police produced Di Bernardo at a press conference with the intention of discrediting the human rights organizations that had, in all good faith, denounced his supposed disappearance after his faked abduction had been reported both to them and in a sworn statement before a judge, the full story was officially withheld. In a memorandum issued by CELS on February 2, 1982, the complete details of the case were made public. In the meantime, a federal judge ordered the prosecution of the human rights workers involved in the case, charging them with breaking a law that provides prison terms of between five and twenty-five years for any Argentine citizen who "proposed political or economic sanctions against the state." This was merely the most recent case within a series of attempts by the government to discredit human rights organizations by falsely charging them with fabricating abductions and then harassing them with police raids, investigations, and criminal prosecutions.

Taming the Wild Things

It is difficult to recapture what it feels like to live in a state of total terrorism. The mind resists the illogicality of remembrances of past fears. Argentina may not be a unique case of a society beleaguered by so many and so varied forms of terrorism, but it is certainly an extreme case. Perhaps there are some lessons to be learned from the way people live in a society close to the limits of bearable stress.

One characteristic of Argentina throughout the 1970s was the compulsion to minimize everything, to refuse to notice disturbing trends until they became absolutely overwhelming.

I had five children growing up during Argentina's years of total terrorism. My eldest child was born in 1962 and the youngest in 1971, so that our lives were fraught with fear on their behalf throughout the 1970s. Terror reigned throughout the decade, claiming the lives of at least twenty thousand people.

Looking back now, it strikes me that the best way to capture the atmosphere of those times is to describe the children's book that I read to all of them as they grew up. It was sent to me from England by my sister, who has a doctorate in education and specializes in the teaching of very young children.

I do not think her choice of the book was a conscious effort to help the children live through terrorism. The book was, and is, popular all over the world. It is *Where the Wild Things Are* by Maurice Sendak. It was a perfect book for children growing up with terrorism because it takes the fear out of fearsome things. It is a book of wild, crazy monsters, thumping great creatures summoned up from the most terrible depths of the imagination. And it tells of a boy who tames into drooling submission the most terrible wild things—fabulous griffinlike creatures with huge teeth and talons and horrendous mythical beasts, part dragon, part crocodile but elephantine in size. The book turns every horrendous beast that has ever haunted young dreams into a pet. It is a wonderful book to tame terrors, and the children and I delighted in it.

Looking back now, I see that book, which was probably therapeutic for my children, as a paradigm of the Argentine reaction to terrorism. From the very start of the terrorist assault on Argentine society, people responded by trying to evade facing up to the challenge it posed to them. I have come to think that the most terrifying thing about terrorism is the way people can so easily come to accept it and justify it, even perhaps, like my children with the tamed monsters in Maurice Sendak's book, to enjoy a vicarious thrill from violence they thought would never touch them.

I recall taking a taxi one morning in 1972, when the wild ones enjoyed considerable popularity and were called guerrillas. I can see the grinning face of the driver still, as he turned back to me, while swerving through the mad rush of Buenos Aires traffic rounding the obelisk, to say:

"Well, they got another one!"

"Another what?" I asked him.

"Another cop," he said with relish.

"Every time they get another one, I dance for joy," he said.

I made no comment. His outlook was fairly common at that time.

But it was not typical. The majority of people did not rejoice in murder. They simply accepted violence as part of life, hoping, and largely believing, that they would not be affected by it.

Terrorism to those who believed that they could never be its victims, because they were not policemen, members of the armed forces, judges, top government officials, rich businessmen, or rich foreigners, was something to be accepted, even justified. In their minds, they tamed the wild things loose in Argentine society in much the same way as Maurice Sendak's drawings drained away the horror from monsters in the imagination of my children.

I remember how, during a rash of kidnapping of businessmen, a good friend, a young Anglo-Argentine woman who was a private secretary, justified these kidnappings. She explained to me that many Argentine businessmen evaded taxes. Therefore it was reasonable that they should be made to pay in ransom what they failed to pay in tribute. This was a variation of the pestilent romanticism of Robin Hood and the continuation of the myth that the terrorist groups in Argentina were robbing the rich to give to the poor.

At the same time the attitude of the government was to play down the importance of the guerrillas. Intense pressure was put upon the media to avoid reporting the full extent of the terrorism. The People's Revolutionary Army (ERP), for example, actually held territory in Argentina, an area where they ruled for over a year before any serious efforts were made to deal with the threat they presented. Throughout this time, the national media also kept clear of the area, never reporting upon it. And reports that appeared abroad were dismissed as being exaggerated or "anti-Argentine" propaganda. The general attitude of everyone up until Christmas of 1974 when Peron's widow, Isabelita, ordered the army into Tucuman to take on the ERP, was that Argentina could never become violent. Argentina's terrorists were looked upon as being different.

Sowing the Dragon's Teeth

Shortly after the military takeover, *Gente*, the most popular weekly newsmagazine in Argentina, published a book. Titled *Photos-Events-Testimonies of 1035 Dramatic Days*,[10] it purported to tell the story of the government that had just been overthrown. In actual fact, the book set out to tell the story it had assiduously avoided telling while the events in question were taking place. Into the book went the material that the editors of *Gente* had rigorously self-censored before.

For some years now, reality in Argentina has been possible only after the event. While the Peronist government was in power, *Gente* published the stories and printed the pictures that the government wanted to see. When the military took over, *Gente* set out to report the news the way the new government wanted it, displaying marked enthusiasm for the military. Although embarrassingly eulogistic about Peron, its support for

10. (Buenos Aires: Editorial Atlantida, 1976.)

his government was always grudging. To a greater or lesser degree, depending upon economic interests and political loyalties, the entire Argentine press does the same. (Television and radio are largely owned and strictly controlled by the government.) Public indignation, therefore, is always being whipped into a frenzy long after the die has been cast.

The media's coverage of terrorism followed this pattern. While terrorism was at its height, the press was minimizing its perils, although very often dangerously glamorizing its exploits.[11] Foreign correspondents were criticized for exaggerating the violence in Argentina. When the military took over and the press was encouraged to tell readers how bad things really had been, another, different, wave of terrorism—that of the state security apparatus—was going unreported. Then foreign correspondents were criticized for not rereporting the events they had been asked to hush up while they were taking place.

By March 1976, when the military took power, the tide in the battle against terrorism had probably turned. A series of successful takeovers (never more than a few hours in duration) of military installations, which grabbed headlines but probably did more than anything else to alert the armed forces to the threat to their survival posed by the terrorists, had caused both the major groups, the left-wing Peronist Montoneros and the Marxist-Leninist People's Revolutionary Army, to overreach themselves. Both had received crushing reverses when they attacked military garrisons that had finally got round to taking special security measures (triple sentries, for example, with each man standing sentinel over another). But much more was at stake than merely crushing the terrorists.

The figures relating to murders carried out by terrorists were

11. Andrew Graham-Yooll, *Portrait of an Exile* (London: Junction Books, 1981), captures the atmosphere of this period and, particularly, the relationship between the press and the terrorist organizations. Graham-Yooll was news editor and political columnist of the *Buenos Aires Herald* until, upon instinct, he decided to leave Argentina in September 1976. I later learned that he was, incredibly, on the list of terrorist suspects kept by one of the secret kidnapping groups within the security apparatus. If he had remained in Argentina, it is probable that both he and his wife would have "disappeared."

inflated from the start and have invariably included the victims of the security forces. Nevertheless, the toll taken by terrorism was so high that it was always clear that counterterrorism would have a massive input of vengeance. The most reliable official figures claim that the terrorists killed between five hundred and seven hundred people up to the end of 1979.[12] More than half this number were military personnel. Among the military men assassinated were five army generals, two admirals, and, from the air force, a brigadier and four commodores. More than 347 police were killed, including three federal police chiefs.

The wife of one general was ruthlessly slain after her husband had been assassinated. A lieutenant who was ambushed and murdered died alongside his seven-year-old daughter, while his other child, a girl of five, was critically wounded. The terrorists, in placing a bomb in an empty apartment immediately below the home of the navy commander in chief, killed his sixteen-year-old daughter and an old lady of seventy-nine.[13]

It is not surprising that one of the army commanders, whose sister was killed by terrorists, was known—and mightily

12. *El terrorismo en la Argentina* gives a total of 596 assassinations up to September 1979. (Since then there have been three more murders by left-wing terrorists.) But this list includes a number of murders or disappearances that cannot be attributed to leftist extremists. Among the victims named is Hector Hidalgo Sola, appointed Argentine ambassador to Venezuela by the military, whose family is convinced that his disappearance was the work of the security forces. Elena Holmberg, another Argentine diplomat ideologically identified with the military regime, who was found murdered just before Christmas 1978, is also included in the official list of victims of terrorism. Her family believes that she was kidnapped and murdered by a secret navy commando unit because of rivalry between the army and navy commanders. In a recent report in *Human Events* ("How Argentina Won Its War against Leftist Terrorism," February 13, 1982, p. 10), Virginia Prewitt and William R. Mizelle cite a figure of 688 deaths up to the end of 1979. But they fudge the issue of responsibility by attributing them to "homicidal shadow-forces."

13. A highly personal and finely written memoir by Eduardo Galeano, *Dias y noches de amor y de guerra* (Barcelona: Editorial Laia, 1978), provides some moving insights into the atmosphere of fear in Buenos Aires when the counterterrorist offensive of the armed forces got under way. Galeano writes from the point of view of someone who knew that he was "on the list" of the right-wing abduction groups and death squads from the start. His book provides an interesting counterpoint to Andrew Graham-Yooll's treatment of some similar events.

feared—as "El Vengador" (the Avenger) and that the mentality of the counterterrorist forces came to resemble that of the terrorists themselves.

The Heart of the Nightmare

I believe that it is very important to try to understand how techniques so similar to Hitler's "night and fog" policy of liquidation came to be applied in Argentina. Perhaps it is tendentious to speak of Nazi techniques. The disappearances reminded me, from the start, of KGB methods. It was particularly disturbing to find oneself picking up in the Argentina of 1976–79 echoes of atrocities committed long ago and far away. The Swedish ambassador in Argentina at that time, who became a good friend, had spent much of his diplomatic career in Russia. When I told him that the Argentine security forces were using closed vans, disguised to resemble the vehicles in which wholesale groceries are delivered, to abduct people (or, to use a phrase that was coined by human rights workers, "to disappear people"), he recalled that during Stalin's purges victims were carted off in trucks used to deliver bread.

Some among the few lucky enough to emerge from secret detention camps, usually because they had agreed to try to rejoin terrorist organizations they had been associated with and report back to the security forces, revealed that victims who were to be liquidated (the routine method was to drug them and throw them unconscious from aircraft into the Atlantic) were always told that they were being transferred to a "far better place." In several of the camps, prisoners were encouraged to believe that if they cooperated and worked with the guards, even, in some cases, assisting at torture sessions, they would be rewarded by being sent south to a farm camp. There is, however, no evidence that any such places existed. Stories still circulate among relatives of disappeared people about secret rehabilitation camps. The military did establish a small retraining center, housing less than a score of people, for terrorists who turned themselves in. Local journalists and foreign human rights delegations have been allowed to visit this facility.

This is the sole example of humane treatment being accorded to convicted terrorists. Of course, because the Argentine military government has never admitted holding terrorist suspects outside the framework of the law, there has never been any accountability.

The disappearances are the heart of the Argentine nightmare, the core of its tragedy. It is difficult for the mind to grasp their awesome significance. It is a problem as complex and baffling as Rubik's cube but there is no satisfaction to be had in grappling with it because there is no prospect of solution while the military maintain the attitude they have assumed since the outset of their counterattack against terrorism just before the March 1976 coup.

The official response has changed over the years. At the height of the disappearances, the official line was that there were no disappearances. If an explanation had to be given to outsiders (the Argentine press knew, instinctively, not to ask), it followed this formula:

In a "dirty war" like that being fought against terrorism, the lines of battle are never clearly drawn. The bodies of people killed in explosions are often unrecognizable. The terrorists themselves carried out executions of their own comrades for various reasons. Many terrorists fled abroad. Others shed their identity to escape from the clutches of terrorist organizations they no longer wanted to be associated with.

This formula reply was so unconvincing that, for foreign consumption, at least, the military leaders admitted that it was possible that some disappearances could have resulted from "excesses" committed by members of the security forces. As foreign concern strengthened the tiny band of people concerned about human rights in Argentina, questions began to be asked at home as well as abroad, and the military response evolved again. It is now tacitly acknowledged that people have disappeared. Those disappearances cannot be explained. Nevertheless, the official line goes, the disappearances have helped to restore peace to Argentina.

It is as if the United States, having dropped atom bombs on Hiroshima and Nagasaki, had denied all knowledge of the matter. The disappearances in Argentina, allied with other ruthless methods, undoubtedly exterminated the terrorists—along with some totally innocent people and a great many others who were only marginally involved in terrorism. Yet, because the government refuses to acknowledge that it used the technique, there can be no discussion or debate about its efficacy, let alone its comparative morality, and no compassion, sympathy, or reparation for innocent victims. It forces those who support the government to make a contract with lies and deceit. The consequences of this problem without a solution hardly bear thinking about.

It is not easy to come up for air with any rational conclusions after being plunged like a torture victim into the fetid waters of Argentine terrorism and counterterrorism. For a start, a vein of irrationality runs through recent Argentine history.

There was no justification for the escalation of terror by the left wing in Argentina. The Peronist left wing had been granted legitimacy through the elections of March 1973, and although their representatives in the government were the victims of the purge ordered by Peron upon his return to Argentina, that was more the consequence of the refusal of the guerrilla-cum-terrorist organizations to operate within the system than of attacks from the traditional fascists of the Peronist right wing. The left-right polarization within the Peronist movement was exacerbated by the aggressiveness of the Montoneros. The left chose violence and played into the hands of the Peronist right wing, which controlled the masses through the Peronist trade unions.

Despite the political stridency of the Peronist Youth, Argentina's young people were really enrolled in the worldwide youth revolution of the 1960s, which, like so many other ideas and fashions, arrived a little late in Argentina. Many of the victims of the security forces' kidnapping and death squads were young people with only a peripheral involvement in the violent politics of the time. The security forces, when they carted away the bodies after the murder squads had been in action, called them "perejil," which means, literally, "parsley." (To use an English expression, they were very small potatoes, indeed.)

The appeal of Cuba was romantic, and although most of the major guerrilla/terrorist leaders were given training at some time or other in Cuba, there is no evidence to support military claims that massive aid was provided by Havana. Military propaganda consistently sought to play down the Peronist credentials of the young left, but they looked upon themselves as true Peronists. The military were, wisely, intent on using nationalism to counter the appeal of the Peronist new left, so they exaggerated the links with international communism and played down their declared allegiance to Peron. (The Peron that the Young Peronists believed in was a figment of their own imagination—they had an image in their mind of a revolutionary like Chairman Mao, and they closed their eyes to the reality of the ailing, ancient fascist even when he turned on them. They blamed his wife and Lopez Rega for the open scorn he showed for them.)

The counterterrorist campaign of the armed forces was equally emotional and irrational. Their escalation of terror is best explained as the consequence of inefficiency. The security forces were so inept in dealing with terrorism that they were driven by desperation to extreme methods and found themselves mimicking the terrorists. Because they operated in total secrecy—and their brutal methods created such an atmosphere of fear that few people would even acknowledge their existence—the security groups responsible for assassinations and disappearances never had to account for their actions and were not held responsible for them. This led to a parallel wave of criminality, with robbery accompanying kidnapping, which also tightened up the screws of terror.

Both terrorists and terroristic counterterrorists claimed that their methods were justified by circumstances. The Argentine military, when explaining their actions in private, often sounded like the Nazis, who argued that because the world could never be told of their "final solution" for "the Jewish problem," the nobility of their actions was even greater because their sacrifices for the fatherland could never be publicly honored and rewarded. Mariano Grondona, then Argentina's most influential political journalist, and a longtime adviser and facile philosopher for the Argentine military in their interventions in government, once told me that he thought that if I made an effort I would understand the underlying nobility of the armed forces in their "dirty war." "If you think about it," he told me, "it is better to be killed than to have to kill." Several military officers expressed a similar outlook to me when they told me that while they did not like the methods that were being used and did not know how history would judge them, they felt that they must be totally identified with those who had to carry out "the dirty work." They expressed a perverse admiration for men who had done such terrible things that they could not bring themselves to kiss their own children.

The same cult of horror existed among the terrorists. They openly glorified murder (see the accounts of the murder of Admiral Hermes Quijada and of General Pedro Aramburu).[14] But while the atrocities carried out by the terrorists were made known, the equally nefarious activities of the security forces were covered up. As a journalist, my major problem was to establish what was happening. To do that, simply to record events, I went out and did my own reporting. If I had asked one of the reporters to cover what became known as "human

14. A series of articles, "Revolutionary Chronicles," appeared fortnightly for 18 months in 1973 and 1974 in *Liberación por la patria socialista*. Issue 19 (April 17–May 3, 1974) carried the inside story of the murder of Rear Admiral Hermes Quijada by the "ERP 22 Agosto," a splinter group of the ERP formed to avenge the August 22, 1972, deaths of 16 convicted terrorists killed when they tried to stage a jail break from the Navy base in Trelew. *La Causa Peronista,* Sept. 3, 1974, carried an account by the kidnappers of General Pedro Aramburo, who was killed June 1, 1970, by the Montoneros. The complete text of this account was published in English by *Gente* in May, 1978.

rights" ("human rights" came to be a euphemism for murders and other atrocities carried out by members of the security forces, and reporting such matters was considered to be "subversive"), I would have been asking him to risk his life. With each event that was recorded, however, it became easier, and less dangerous, to report other things that were not supposed to be happening. For over a year, other newspapers in Buenos Aires refused to publish reports of kidnappings, even when denounced by relatives of the victims. When distraught parents went to newspapers to report the disappearance of a child, for example, they were told that such incidents could not be published without official authorization or were given patently false excuses—a popular evasion was to claim that the news editor was ill and was the only person who could make a decision on such an important matter.

I came to feel that the worst aspect of the total terrorism that held Argentina in its thrall from 1969 to 1979 was the denial of reality. There were times when I thought that because so many people in Argentina did not want to know what was happening, the facts about the disappearances and the entire apparatus of state terrorism would never become known and that the terror would continue and become part of life in Argentina. Kafka's world of frighteningly realistic unreality came into being and still exists in regard to the netherworld where so many thousands of people have quite simply disappeared. And that impossible, unacceptable explanation is accepted quite simply by many Argentines, even today, when few of them can claim anymore that they do not know what the word "disappearance" implies although they still resist the effort of imagination required to understand its unutterably sinister meaning.

Martha Crenshaw

8

Conclusions

In the words of Irving Louis Horowitz, "terrorism has become a mode of doing politics." It is difficult to generalize broadly about its effects; the problem is subtle, complex, and closely related to particular historical, social, and political contexts. Judgments about the consequences of terrorism presented here are measured and careful. Although Horowitz notes that it is impossible to construct sound policy without an awareness of its social and political effects, he would surely heed Yehezkel Dror's warning: "Our ignorance far surpasses our knowledge."

No single ideology inspires terrorism. It is not the exclusive province of revolutionaries and certainly is not directed in all its ubiquitous manifestations by minions of the Soviet Union. Horowitz argues that it is not useful to speak of "left" and "right" terrorism because in reality the motives and goals of terrorist organizations represent a mixture of ideologies. Most are antistatist and antidemocratic, but there is little other common denominator. Conor Cruise O'Brien emphasizes, for example, that the roots of the IRA lie in Ireland's past, not in international movements. We cannot easily classify the IRA as traditionally "left" or "right." Many similar organizations are more nationalistic or sectarian than revolutionary. (Horowitz argues that nationalists are more likely to succeed, a finding that O'Brien and Paul Wilkinson would dispute.) Furthermore, as Wilkinson demonstrates in the case of Northern Ireland, violence by the Protestant defenders of the old order, who wish to restore an autonomous Ulster under Protestant domination, is as intractable a problem for British policy-makers as the terrorism of the IRA. Each extremism depends on the other in a bizarre sort of violent symbiosis.

Most of these writers remind us that terrorists strike not only against the state but also on its behalf. We should be concerned by the terrorism of civilian proponents of a past or present status quo, as well as by the terrorism of governments. Some states, like the Argentina of 1976 to 1979 that Robert Cox describes, employ counterterrorism against a perceived threat from revolutionary forces. The terrorism of the government far exceeds in magnitude and impact on society the violence of its challengers. Terrorism by the state against its own citizens is not limited to a specific historical time or place—such as Nazi Germany and the Soviet Union in the interwar period. It may indeed be commonplace.

The use of terrorism as a foreign policy tool by states is a recent development in international politics. Regimes such as Iran and Libya use terrorism against both domestic dissidents and foreign opponents. Anthony Quainton and Dror recommend that democratic states consistently oppose this alarming trend, if necessary with concrete sanctions.

While perhaps not openly or directly employing terrorism, governments sometimes manipulate terrorist organizations for their own purposes. The experiences of Argentina contain a lesson for other governments. Peron, before his return to power in 1973, encouraged Montonero terrorism against the Campora government. When he assumed power, he discovered that he could not control the forces he had encouraged from exile. After the "left" of the Peronist movement split from the "right," terrorism escalated to the point of provoking a military coup against Peron's widow.

These authors agree that governments must learn to adapt to terrorism because it is likely to be a permanent feature of politics among and within nations. Expansion rather than contraction of terrorist activity is generally expected. Cautiously admitting only the possibility, not the probability, of increasing terrorism, Dror outlines directions and patterns of change. He argues that it is better to be prepared for terrorism that does not occur than unprepared for terrorism that does. Yet democratic states find it difficult to formulate long-run goals for antiterrorist policy. This reluctance or incapacity to construct an appropriate response may stem from a combination of factors: domestic politics, the difficulty of making value judgments about political violence, the unpredictability of terrorism, or its unforeseeable and often unanticipated consequences. Dror urges that policy be sequentially and incrementally developed and reevaluated periodically in light of changing events.

Anthony Quainton points out that one of the keystones of American policy toward terrorism is the concept of deterrence.[1] It is important that governments, and perhaps private actors as well, not reward terrorists. Some questions may be raised, however, about the viability of the option of deterrence, which is an attempt to influence the choices of terrorist organizations before they are made by affecting calculations of reward and punishment. Although the goal of preventing terrorism by affecting terrorist motivations is laudable, governments and terrorist organizations may not share the same standards of rationality. The structure of costs and benefits may not be identical to both parties. Threats to deny the satisfaction of ostensible demands such as the release of prisoners or payment of monetary ransom may mean less to terrorists than to the government. Punishment in the form of death or imprisonment may not deter an individual who values martyrdom in the service of a transcendental cause, such as the ideal of a united Ireland. Nor do assumptions that deterrence is effective consider what happens when deterrence fails or provide a means for determining when it has succeeded.

1. The other policy elements, aptly summarized by Quainton, are law enforcement, social and economic reform, moral suasion, and media restraint.

Few decision-makers appear to have assessed the costs associated with different responses to terrorism, comparing them to the costs of nonresponse. Dror states that the costs of responding to terrorism are not high but does not provide detailed explanation. An evaluation of costs, broadly conceived to include political and social as well as financial consequences, should be combined with analysis of policy effectiveness. Is the undoubtedly high monetary cost of maintaining special military or police intervention units in a state of constant readiness worthwhile compared to the frequency of use and effectiveness of forceful intervention in hostage-taking episodes? Is the use of surveillance techniques worth their cost to individual freedom and privacy?

A focus on terrorism should not blind policy-makers to other political, social, and economic problems. However compelling the search for a solution may seem, it must be placed in perspective. Terrorism is not the most important problem modern governments face. Issues of the economy, arms control, and social welfare rank higher than terrorism in the priorities of most Western governments. The allotment of resources to suppressing terrorism must be considered in light of competing interests. Dror recommends that we think of terrorism as another policy problem and that procedures for coping with it be conceived in terms of their general utility in handling other crises. Terrorism is not an isolated phenomenon; it is one of many challenges to the democratic state.

Terrorism as a domestic problem for liberal states is more of a threat to democracy than to stability. Horowitz agrees with Dror in concluding that democratic states may be weakened but not dealt mortal blows by terrorism. He cites Israel as a particular example.[2] That terrorism thrives in democracies does not mean that underneath liberal facades lies oppression

2. For a critical analysis of Israeli policy, see Hanan Alon, *Countering Palestinian Terrorism in Israel: Toward a Policy Analysis of Countermeasures* (Santa Monica: Rand, 1980). See also Paul Wilkinson, *Terrorism and the Liberal State* (New York: Wiley, 1977); and J. Bowyer Bell, *A Time of Terror: How Democratic Societies Respond to Revolutionary Violence* (New York: Basic Books, 1978).

or that such afflicted regimes are unstable (just as the absence of terrorism does not necessarily indicate a state of justice). Although Wilkinson, O'Brien, and Quainton are less sanguine about terrorism's implications for democratic stability, they would agree that Great Britain, West Germany, Italy, Spain, and Israel have successfully withstood high levels of terrorism.

Horowitz proposes that terrorism has more to do with limits on civil liberties than with the preservation of the institutions of government and urges that protecting democracy is more essential than maintaining order. The threat of terrorism is not grave enough to justify the establishment of garrison states in a neofeudal system. Quainton and O'Brien agree that legitimacy is the key to the successful response to terrorism. In this respect, Robert Cox reminds us that the absence of political accountability is immensely dangerous. In a situation such as existed in Argentina, where terrorists singled out the military and police as targets, an ominous combination of embittering vengeance and frustrating inefficiency led security forces to counterterrorism. Anonymity and secrecy were not compatible with democratic policies.

Terrorism is more a foreign than a domestic issue for the United States; for states like Japan, Israel, and West Germany, it has been a threat on both levels. Yet the severity of terrorism as an international problem seems to have decreased over the past decade. The reasons for the decline in hijackings and diplomatic kidnappings remain obscure. We do not know whether government policies of prevention and deterrence have been effective or whether terrorist organizations have changed their strategies. Therefore we cannot predict the prospects for decline or resurgence. Governments must be prepared without knowing precisely what it is they are preparing for. The danger, as with most military planning, is of being prepared for the last war and thus oblivious to new conceptions of warfare.

In the formation of international policy, governments cannot rely on a significantly higher degree of interstate cooperation than exists today. States seem unlikely to unite further in the struggle against terrorism, in part because the threat appears to be fading. As a foreign policy measure, governments might find it more useful to avoid confronting the controversial issue of terrorism head-on and to try instead to restrict the technological means open to terrorists. Governments could do more to reduce "the ready availability of the tools of the trade," in Quainton's words. International cooperation could affect future terrorism substantially, and in a way critical to the general potential for international conflict, by establishing safeguards for special nuclear materials and by controlling conventional arms transfers.[3]

Although Horowitz is right in noting that the impact of modern terrorism must be measured on a worldwide basis, ultimately terrorism has not changed the nature of power or its configuration in international relations. It has not resulted in significant territorial changes in the postwar period, unless one counts the independence struggles that resulted in the creation of Israel and Algeria. Since 1918 it has not precipitated, much less caused, world war, although it has aggravated regional conflict in the Middle East. In the 1970s, primarily under the impact of economic developments and the oil crisis, many analysts suspected that international relations would become transnational relations as nonstate actors gained influence and as the legitimacy and power of the nation-state declined.[4] Multinational corporations and revolutionary movements were thought to be the heirs to the antiquated state in the new world order of interdependence. As Quainton and Horowitz observe, terrorism has facilitated interdependence. The state, however, has resisted its demise. Terrorism appears to have strengthened the old order, underscored the primacy of force in international relations, and even highlighted the centrality of the Cold War confrontation between the United States and the Soviet Union,

3. This is a point also made by Garry Brewer, who cited terrorism as one contributor to an insecure future world: *Existing in a World of Institutionalized Danger* (New Haven: Yale University, School of Organization and Management, Technical Report No. 102, March 1976).

4. Robert O. Keohane and Joseph S. Nye, Jr., eds., *Transnational Relations and World Politics* (Cambridge, Mass.: Harvard University Press, 1971), represents an early example of this school of thought.

at whose door the United States lays the blame for sponsoring global subversion. The major risk of international conflict perhaps lies less in revolutionary terrorism against the state than in the state use or exploitation of terrorism as an instrument of foreign policy.

In sum, for governments terrorism adds to the complexity of the political and social environment. Like many other ill-defined and imperfectly understood problems, it has no easy solution. Dror finds it improbable and perhaps even unnecessary for governments to develop new and bold policies for controlling terrorism unless there is dramatic expansion. He suspects that radical policy changes would probably be inefficient anyway, because they could not be integrated with the existing procedures that have so far worked well. Policy-makers must learn to adjust to indeterminacy and uncertainty. Incidents of terrorism are typically modern forms of international crisis: messy, rapid, and complicated. John Keegan, in a critical analysis of the political management of military power, warns that the attributes of the Cuban missile crisis—neatness, simplicity, and "the velocity of chess"—are not likely to recur. "Much more likely is an altogether messier set of events in which the velocities of riot, terrorism, and the selfish and unreflecting acts of third parties will jog the elbows of the great, forcing them to take decisions at a pace too fast for them to calculate all, or even many, of the consequences."[5]

5. "The Human Face of Deterrence," *International Security* 6 (Summer 1981): 146.

Selected Bibliography

Agirre, Julen. *Operation Ogro*. Translated by Barbara P. Solomon. New York: Ballantine, 1975.

Alexander, Yonah, ed. *International Terrorism: National, Regional, and Global Perspectives*. New York: Praeger, 1976.

——, Browne, Marjorie, and Nanes, Allan S., eds. *Control of Terrorism: International Documents*. New York: Crane, Russak, 1979.

——, Carlton, David, and Wilkinson, Paul, eds. *Terrorism: Theory and Practice*. Boulder: Westview, 1979.

——, and Finger, Seymour Maxwell, eds. *Terrorism: Interdisciplinary Perspectives*. New York: John Jay Press, 1977.

——, and Gleason, John M., eds. *Behavioral and Quantitative Perspectives on Terrorism*. New York: Pergamon, 1981.

—— and Kilmarx, Robert A., eds. *Political Terrorism and Business: The Threat and Response*. New York: Praeger, 1979.

Alon, Hanan. *Countering Palestinian Terrorism in Israel: Toward a Policy Analysis of Countermeasures*. Santa Monica: Rand, 1980.

Apter, David E. "Notes on the Underground: Left Violence and the National State." *Daedalus* 108 (Fall 1979): 155–72.

Arblaster, Anthony. "Terrorism: Myths, Meaning and Morals." *Political Studies* 25 (1977): 413–24.

Baldwin, David A. "Bargaining with Airline Hijackers." In *The 50% Solution*, edited by I. William Zartman, pp. 404–29. Garden City, N.Y.: Doubleday, 1976.

Baumann, Carol Edler. *The Diplomatic Kidnappings: A Revolutionary Tactic of Urban Terrorism*. The Hague: Nijhoff, 1973.

Becker, Jillian. *Hitler's Children: The Story of the Baader-Meinhof Terrorist Gang*. Philadelphia: J. B. Lippincott, 1977.

Begin, Menachem. *The Revolt*. Translated by Samuel Katz. Rev. ed. Los Angeles: Nash, 1977.

Bell, J. Bowyer. "Assassination in International Politics: Lord Moyne, Count Bernadotte, and Lehi." *International Studies Quarterly* 16 (March 1972): 59–82.

——. *The Secret Army: A History of the IRA, 1916–1979*. Cambridge: M.I.T. Press, 1980.

——. *Terror out of Zion: Irgun, LEHI, and the Palestine Underground, 1929–1949*. New York: St. Martin's Press, 1976.

——. *A Time of Terror: How Democratic Societies Respond to Revolutionary Violence*. New York: Basic Books, 1978.

——. *Transnational Terror*. Washington and Stanford: American Enterprise Institute/Hoover Institution, 1975.

——. "Trends on Terror: The Analysis of Political Violence." *World Politics* 19 (April 1977): 476–88.

Bell, J. Bowyer, and Gurr, Ted Robert. "Terrorism and Revolution in America." In *Violence in America: Historical and Comparative*

Perspectives, edited by Hugh Davis Graham and Ted Robert Gurr, pp. 329–47. Rev. ed. Beverly Hills: Sage, 1979.

Bell, Robert G. "The U.S. Response to Terrorism against International Civil Aviation." *Orbis* 19 (Winter 1976): 1326–43.

Beres, Louis René. "Guerrillas, Terrorists, and Polarity: New Structural Models of World Politics." *Western Political Quarterly* 27 (December 1974): 624–36.

———. *Terrorism and Global Security: The Nuclear Threat*. Boulder: Westview, 1979.

Blair, Bruce G., and Brewer, Garry D. "The Terrorist Threat to World Nuclear Programs." *Journal of Conflict Resolution* 21 (September 1977): 379–403.

Bloomfield, Louis M., and Fitzgerald, Gerald F. *Crimes against Internationally Protected Persons: Prevention and Punishment*. New York: Praeger, 1975.

Bonanate, Luigi. "Some Unanticipated Consequences of Terrorism." *Journal of Peace Research* 16 (1979): 192–212.

Bowden, Tom. "The IRA and the Changing Tactics of Terrorism." *Political Quarterly* 47 (October–December 1976): 425–37.

Brooks, Roy L. "Skyjacking and Refugees: The Effect of the Hague Convention upon Asylum." *Harvard International Law Journal* 16 (Winter 1975): 93–112.

Buckley, Alan D., and Olson, Daniel D., eds. *International Terrorism: Current Research and Future Directions*. Wayne, N.J.: Avery Publishing Group, 1980.

Burton, Anthony. *Urban Terrorism: Theory, Practice and Response*. New York: Free Press, 1975.

Clutterbuck, Richard. *Guerrillas and Terrorists*. London: Faber and Faber, 1977.

———. *Living with Terrorism*. London: Faber and Faber, 1975.

Cohen, Geula. *Woman of Violence: Memoirs of a Young Terrorist, 1943–1948*. Translated by Hille Halkin. New York: Holt, Rinehart, and Winston, 1966.

Corsi, Jerome R. "Terrorism as a Desperate Game: Fear, Bargaining, and Communication in the Terrorist Event." *Journal of Conflict Resolution* 25 (March 1981): 47–86.

Cox, Robert. *The Sound of One Hand Clapping: A Preliminary Study of the Argentine Press in a Time of Terror*. Washington: Woodrow Wilson International Center for Scholars, 1980. Working Paper No. 83 of the Latin American Program.

Crelinsten, Ronald D., Laberge-Altmejd, Danielle, and Szabo, Denis. *Terrorism and Criminal Justice: An International Perspective*. Lexington, Mass.: D. C. Heath, 1978.

Crenshaw, Martha. "The Causes of Terrorism." *Comparative Politics* 13 (July 1981): 379–99.

de Boer, Connie. "The Polls: Terrorism and Hijacking." *Public Opinion Quarterly* 43 (Autumn 1979): 410–19.

Dobson, Christopher, and Payne, Ronald. *The Terrorists: Their Weapons, Leaders and Tactics.* Rev. ed. New York: Facts on File, 1982.

Dugard, John. "International Terrorism: Problems of Definition." *International Affairs* 50 (January 1974): 67–81.

Ellsburg, Daniel. *The Theory and Practice of Blackmail.* Santa Monica: Rand, 1968.

Evans, Alona E. "Aircraft Hijacking: What Is Being Done?" *American Journal of International Law* 67 (October 1973): 641–71.

————, and Murphy, John F., eds. *Legal Aspects of International Terrorism.* Lexington, Mass.: D. C. Heath, 1978.

Evans, Ernest. *Calling a Truce to Terror: The American Response to International Terrorism.* Westport, Conn.: Greenwood Press, 1979.

Federal Republic of Germany. Bundesministerium des Innern. *Analysen zum Terrorismus.* 2 vols. Opladen: Westdeutscher Verlag, 1981. Vol. 1: *Ideologien und Strategien,* by Iring Fetscher and Günter Rohrmoser. Vol. 2: *Lebenslaufanalysen,* by Herbert Jäger, Gerhard Schmidtchen, and Lieselotte Süllvold.

Fetscher, Iring. *Terrorismus und Reaktion.* Cologne: Europäische Verlangsanstalt, 1977.

Figner, Vera. *Mémoires d'une révolutionnaire.* Translated by Victor Serge. Paris: Gallimard, 1930.

Franck, Thomas M., and Lockwood, Bert B., Jr. "Preliminary Thoughts toward an International Convention on Terrorism." *American Journal of International Law* 68 (January 1974): 69–90.

Fromkin, David. "The Strategy of Terrorism." *Foreign Affairs* 53 (July 1975): 683–98.

Funke, Manfred, ed. *Terrorismus: Untersuchungen zur Struktur und Strategie revolutionärer Gewaltpolitik.* Dusseldorf: Athenaeum, 1977.

Gaucher, Roland. *Les terroristes.* Paris: Albin Michel, 1965.

Gerasimov, Lt.-Gen. Aleksandr V. *Tsarisme et terrorisme. Souvenirs du Général Guérassimov, ancien chef de l'Okhrana de Saint-Pétersbourg, 1909–1912.* Translated by Thérese Monceaux. Paris: Plon, 1934.

Greisman, H. C. "Social Meanings of Terrorism: Reification, Violence, and Social Control." *Contemporary Crises* 1 (1977): 303–18.

Gross, Feliks. *Violence in Politics: Terror and Political Assassination in Eastern Europe and Russia.* The Hague: Mouton, 1972.

Gross, Leo. "International Terrorism and International Criminal Jurisdiction." *American Journal of International Law* 67 (July 1973): 508–11.

Guttman, David. "Killers and Consumers: The Terrorist and His Audience." *Social Research* 46 (Autumn 1979): 517–26.

Hacker, Frederick J. *Crusaders, Criminals, Crazies: Terror and Terrorism in Our Time.* New York: Norton, 1976.

Halperin, Ernst. *Terrorism in Latin America.* Beverly Hills: Sage, 1976.

Hannay, William M. "International Terrorism and the Political Offense Exception to Extradition." *Columbia Journal of Transnational Law* 18 (1980): 381–412.

Hodges, Donald C., ed. and trans. *Philosophy of the Urban Guerrilla: The Revolutionary Writings of Abraham Guillen.* New York: William Morrow, 1973.

Horowitz, Irving Louis. "Political Terrorism and State Power." *Journal of Political and Military Sociology* 1 (Spring 1973): 147–57.

Horsley, Richard A. "The Sicarii: Ancient Jewish 'Terrorists.'" *Journal of Religion* 59 (October 1979): 435–58.

Husbands, Christopher T. "Contemporary Right-Wing Extremism in Western European Democracies: A Review Article." *European Journal of Political Research* 9 (March 1981): 75–100.

Hutchinson, Martha Crenshaw. "The Concept of Revolutionary Terrorism." *Journal of Conflict Resolution* 16 (September 1972): 383–96.

———. *Revolutionary Terrorism: The FLN in Algeria, 1954–1962.* Stanford: Hoover Institution Press, 1978.

———. "Transnational Terrorism and World Politics." *Jerusalem Journal of International Relations* 1 (Winter 1975): 109–29.

Hyams, Edward. *Terrorists and Terrorism.* New York: St. Martin's Press, 1974.

Ikor, Roger. *Lettre ouverte à de gentils terroristes.* Paris: Albin Michel, 1976.

Iviansky, Ze'ev. "Individual Terror: Concept and Typology." *Journal of Contemporary History* 12 (January 1977): 43–64.

Jackson, Geoffrey. *Surviving the Long Night: An Autobiographical Account of a Political Kidnapping.* New York: Vanguard, 1974.

Jenkins, Brian M. *Embassies under Siege: A Review of 48 Embassy Takeovers, 1971–1980.* Santa Monica: Rand, 1981.

———, Johnson, Janera, and Ronfeldt, David. *Numbered Lives: Some Statistical Observations from 77 International Hostage Episodes.* Santa Monica: Rand, 1977.

Joyner, Nancy Douglas. *Aerial Hijackings as an International Crime.* Dobbs Ferry, N.Y.: Oceana Publications, 1974.

Khaled, Leila. *My People Shall Live: The Autobiography of a Revolutionary.* London: Hodder and Stoughton, 1973.

Kohl, James, and Litt, John, eds. *Urban Guerrilla Warfare in Latin America.* Cambridge, Mass.: M.I.T. Press, 1974.

Kupperman, Robert, and Trent, Darrell. *Terrorism: Threat, Reality, Response.* Stanford: Hoover Institution Press, 1979.

Kuriyama, Yoshihiro. "Terrorism at Tel Aviv Airport and a 'New Left' Group in Japan." *Asian Survey* 13 (March 1973): 336–46.

Kutner, Luis. "Constructive Notice: A Proposal to End International Terrorism." *New York Law Forum* 19 (Fall 1973): 325–50.

Laqueur, Walter. "Interpretations of Terrorism—Fact, Fiction and Political Science." *Journal of Contemporary History* 12 (January 1977): 1–42.

——. *Terrorism: A Study of National and International Political Violence.* Boston: Little, Brown, 1977.

——, ed. *The Terrorism Reader: A Historical Anthology.* Philadelphia: Temple University Press, 1978.

Lee, Alfred McClung. "The Dynamics of Terrorism in Northern Ireland, 1968–1980." *Social Research* 48 (Spring 1981): 100–34.

Lodge, Juliet, ed. *Terrorism: A Challenge to the State.* New York: St. Martin's Press, 1981.

McGuire, Maria. *To Take Arms: My Year with the IRA Provisionals.* New York: Viking, 1973.

MacStiofain, Sean. *Memoirs of a Revolutionary.* N.p.: Gordon Cremonesi, 1975.

Marighela, Carlos. *For the Liberation of Brazil.* Translated by John Butt and Rosemary Sheed. Harmondsworth: Penguin, 1971.

May, W. F. "Terrorism as Strategy and Ecstasy." *Social Research* 41 (Summer 1974): 277–98.

Mickolus, Edward F. *The Literature of Terrorism: A Selectively Annotated Bibliography.* Westport, Conn.: Greenwood Press, 1980.

——. "Negotiating for Hostages: A Policy Dilemma." *Orbis* 19 (Winter 1976): 1309–25.

——. *Transnational Terrorism: A Chronology of Events, 1968–79.* Westport, Conn.: Greenwood Press, 1980.

Midlarsky, Manus I., Crenshaw, Martha, and Yoshida, Fumihiko. "Why Violence Spreads: The Contagion of International Terrorism." *International Studies Quarterly* 24 (June 1980): 262–98.

Miller, Abraham H. *Terrorism and Hostage Negotiations.* Boulder: Westview, 1980.

Morf, Gustave. *Terror in Quebec: Case Studies of the FLQ.* Toronto: Clarke, Irvin, 1970.

Moss, Robert. "International Terrorism and Western Societies." *International Journal* 28 (Summer 1973): 418–30.

Nathan, James A. "The New Feudalism." *Foreign Policy* 42 (Spring 1981): 156–66.

National Advisory Committee on Criminal Justice Standards and Goals. *Disorders and Terrorism.* Report of the Task Force on Disorders and Terrorism, 1976. Washington, D.C.: U.S. Government Printing Office, 1977.

Netanyahu, Benjamin, ed. *International Terrorism: Challenge and Response.* New Brunswick, N.J.: Transaction Books, 1981.

Norton, Augustus R., and Greenberg, Martin H., eds. *Studies in Nuclear Terrorism.* Boston: G. K. Hall, 1979.

O'Brien, Conor Cruise. *Herod: Reflections on Political Violence.* London: Hutchinson, 1978.

——. "Liberty and Terrorism." *International Security* 2 (Fall 1977): 56–67.

Pierre, Andrew J. "The Politics of International Terrorism." *Orbis* 19 (Winter 1976): 1251–69.

Porzecanski, Arturo C. *Uruguay's Tupamaros: The Urban Guerrilla.* New York: Praeger, 1973.

Price, H. Edward, Jr. "The Strategy and Tactics of Revolutionary Terrorism." *Comparative Studies in Society and History* 19 (January 1977): 52–66.

Purnell, Susanna W., and Wainstein, Eleanor S. *The Problems of U.S. Businesses Operating Abroad in Terrorist Environments.* Santa Monica: Rand, 1981.

Rapoport, David C. *Assassination and Terrorism.* Toronto: Canadian Broadcasting Corporation, 1971.

Rapoport, David C., and Alexander, Yonah, eds. *The Morality of Terrorism: Religious and Secular Justifications.* New York: Pergamon, 1982.

Ronchey, Alberto. "Guns and Gray Matter: Terrorism in Italy." *Foreign Affairs* 57 (Spring 1979): 921–40.

Rosenbaum, David M. "Nuclear Terror." *International Security* 1 (Winter 1977): 140–61.

Roucek, Joseph S. "Sociological Elements of a Theory of Terror and Violence." *American Journal of Economics and Sociology* 21 (April 1962): 165–72.

Royal United Services Institute for Defence Studies. *Ten Years of Terrorism: Collected Views.* New York: Crane, Russak, 1979.

Rozakis, Christos L. "Terrorism and the Internationally Protected Persons in the Light of the ILC's Draft Articles." *International and Comparative Law Quarterly* 23 (January 1974): 32–72.

Russell, Charles A., and Miller, H. Bowman. "Profile of a Terrorist." *Military Review* 58 (August 1977): 21–34.

Savinkov, Boris. *Memoirs of a Terrorist.* Translated by Joseph Shaplen. New York: A. & C. Boni, 1931.

Schamis, Gerardo Jorge. *War and Terrorism in International Affairs.* Translated by Danielle Salti. New Brunswick: Transaction Books, 1980.

Schelling, Thomas C. "Thinking about Nuclear Terrorism." *International Security* 6 (Spring 1982): 61–77.

Schlesinger, Philip. "'Terrorism,' the Media, and the Liberal-Democratic State: A Critique of the Orthodoxy." *Social Research* 48 (Spring 1981): 74–99.

Schmid, Alex, and de Graaf, Janny. *Violence as Communication: Insurgent Terrorism and the Western News Media.* Beverly Hills: Sage, 1982.

Schultz, Richard H., Jr., and Sloan, Stephen, eds. *Responding to the Terrorist Threat: Security and Crisis Management.* New York: Pergamon, 1980.

Servier, Jean. *Le terrorisme.* Paris: Presses Universitaires de France, 1979.

Short, K. R. M. *The Dynamite War: Irish-American Bombers in Victorian Britain.* Dublin: Gill and Macmillan, 1979.

Silj, Alessandro. *Never Again without a Rifle: The Origins of Italian Terrorism.* Translated by Salvator Attanasio. New York: Karz, 1979.

Sloan, Stephen. *Simulating Terrorism.* Norman: University of Oklahoma Press, 1981.

Smart, I. M. H. "The Power of Terror." *International Journal* 30 (Spring 1975): 225–37.

Sobel, Lester A., ed. *Political Terrorism.* 2 vols. New York: Facts on File, 1975 and 1978.

Spirodovitch, Alexandre. *Histoire du terrorisme russe.* Translated by Vladimir Lazarewski. Paris: Payot, 1930.

Steinhof, Patricia G. "Portrait of a Terrorist: An Interview with Kozo Okamoto." *Asian Survey* 16 (September 1976): 830–45.

Sterling, Claire. *The Terror Network: The Secret War of International Terrorism.* New York: Reader's Digest Press/Holt, Rinehart, and Winston, 1981.

Stohl, Michael, ed. *The Politics of Terrorism: A Reader in Theory and Practice.* New York: Marcel Dekker, 1979.

"Symposium: Terrorism and the Media." *Indiana Law Journal* 53 (Summer 1978): 619–777.

Terrorism: An International Journal. 1978–82.

Thornton, Thomas P. "Terror as a Weapon of Political Agitation." In *Internal War: Problems and Approaches,* edited by Harry Eckstein, pp. 71–99. New York: Free Press, 1964.

Ulam, Adam B. *In the Name of the People: Prophets and Conspirators in Prerevolutionary Russia.* New York: Viking, 1977.

Walter, Eugene Victor. *Terror and Resistance: A Study of Political Violence.* New York: Oxford University Press, 1969.

———. "Violence and the Process of Terror." *American Sociological Review* 29 (April 1964): 248–57.

Wilkinson, Paul. *The New Fascists.* London: Grant MacIntyre, 1981.

———. *Political Terrorism.* New York: Wiley, 1974.

———. *Terrorism and the Liberal State.* New York: Wiley, 1977.

———. "Three Questions on Terrorism." *Government and Opposition* 8 (Summer 1973): 290–312.

Willrich, Mason, and Taylor, Theodore B. *Nuclear Theft: Risks and Safeguards.* Cambridge, Mass.: Ballinger, 1974.

Wohlstetter, Roberta. "Kidnapping to Win Friends and Influence People." *Survey* 20 (Autumn 1974): 1–40.

Wolf, John B. "Controlling Political Terrorism in a Free Society." *Orbis* 29 (Winter 1976): 1289–1308.

Young, Robert. "Revolutionary Terrorism, Crime and Morality." *Social Theory and Practice* 4 (Fall 1977): 287–302.

Index